Cambridge Elements ≡

Elements in Public Economics
edited by
Robin Boadway
Queen's University
Frank A. Cowell
The London School of Economics and Political Science
Massimo Florio
University of Milan

POLITICAL COMPETITION AND THE STUDY OF PUBLIC ECONOMICS

Stanley L. Winer
Carleton University and CESifo

J. Stephen Ferris
Carleton University

CAMBRIDGE
UNIVERSITY PRESS

Political Competition and the Study of Public Economics

Elements in Public Economics

DOI: 10.1017/9781009006149
First published online: September 2022

Stanley L. Winer
Carleton University and CESifo

J. Stephen Ferris
Carleton University

Author for correspondence: Stanley L. Winer, stanleywiner@cunet.carleton.ca

Abstract: Why is an understanding of political competition essential for the study of public economics and public policy generally? How can political competition be described and understood, and how does it differ from its strictly economic counterpart? What are the implications of the fact that policy proposals in a democracy must always pass a political test? What are the strengths and weaknesses of electoral competition as a mechanism for the allocation of economic resources? Why are tax structures in democratic polities so complicated, and what implications follow from this for normative views about good policy choice? How can the intensity of political competition be measured, why and how does it vary in mature democracies, and what are the consequences? This Element considers how answers to these questions can be approached, while also illustrating some of the interesting theoretical and empirical work that has been done on them.

Keywords: public economics, political competition, electoral competitiveness, political feasibility, political economy

ISBNs: 9781009001694 (PB), 9781009006149 (OC)
ISSNs: 2516-2276 (online), 2516-2268 (print)

Contents

1 Political Economy in the Study of Public Policy

Public policy in a liberal democracy arises as the outcome of competition among political parties for support from a diverse electorate. This process plays a significant role in determining how economic resources are used in both the public and private sectors. In our view, a full understanding of either part of the polity must therefore consider the relationship between political competition and resource use, whether our purpose is to understand actual policy choices, to judge the resulting outcomes from some normative perspective, or to formulate alternatives. Acknowledging political competition as a primary driver of public policy also leads to the study of how political institutions work, and to assessments of how well they work, instead of, or at least in addition to, the study of the setting and consequences of specific policy instruments. An emphasis on institutions follows, for the same reason that acceptance of the market as an allocation mechanism leads the analyst of the public interest to study property rights and market regulation rather than the reasons for particular prices and quantities.

Our purpose in this Element is to outline the components of such a political economy approach to the analysis of public policy while contributing to its development by studying the meaning of political competition and the role it plays.[1] For part of the analysis, we take the degree of competitiveness as given to consider how working within a framework in which policy choices must always pass a political test affects the nature of policy analysis. We also discuss the measurement and implications of changes in its intensity.

A general sense of our approach to the study of public policy can be gained by briefly comparing it to three well-known alternatives.[2] The exchange-contractarian approach is also concerned with the political economy dimensions of public policy, but from a contract-constitutional perspective.[3] While political economy as we conceive of it stresses the study of how electoral competition shapes fiscal systems and other policy instruments, and how specific aspects of the political process can lead to both desirable and undesirable uses of economic resources, this approach focuses on the need for and design of controls that limit the discretionary power of politicians and public administrators from a classical liberal perspective. Controls at the procedural level as well as restrictions on the

---

[1] Background to our analysis is provided by texts and handbooks that combine political economy and public economics. See, for example, Persson and Tabellini (2000), Drazen (2000), Mueller (2003), Cullis and Jones (2009), Hillman (2019), and Congleton, Grofman, and Voigt (2019), among others.

[2] Hamlin (2018) provides an extended comparison.

[3] This tradition originates with Wicksell (1896). The contemporary literature begins with Buchanan and Tullock (1962).

setting of various policy instruments are considered. Work in this tradition is also motivated by a desire to minimize the coercion that must occur when a citizen agrees to be part of a collective enterprise.[4]

In contrast to the political economy and exchange-contractarian approaches, there is no formal role for politics in existing normative approaches to public finance and public economics. In the public finance tradition, emphasis is placed on various criteria for the design of fiscal systems.[5] These include the minimization of the excess burden of taxation that is part of the full cost of public services, the achievement of horizontal and vertical equity among taxpayers, and the principles of good tax administration. The main focus is on the design of policies that strike a reasonable compromise among these sometimes conflicting criteria.

The public finance tradition has been supplanted by the optimal tax or social planning approach, in which the analyst is guided by the results of optimizing a utilitarian social welfare function with respect to a set of exogenously determined policy alternatives, subject to constraints that are understood to be strictly technological – that is, nonpolitical – in nature, including the costliness of identifying the characteristics of taxpayers, the equilibrium structure of the private economy given individual preferences, technology and endowments, and the government budget constraint. Planning of this kind is an attempt to establish an ideal policy structure that can be used to judge the appropriateness of existing policies and as an aid to the design of better ones.[6]

Both public finance and social planning advocate specific fiscal and other policy structures without acknowledging the role of democratic choice. Indeed, for many practitioners of these approaches, it seems fair to say that competitive politics is regarded as something that often gets in the way of better resource allocation and that must, from time to time, be overcome to achieve better policy outcomes. As Scott (1987, 219) put it: "Economists and public finance specialists pay tribute to the idea of competition in the private sector. But competition in the public sector often makes them uneasy."

We view the willingness to plan substantial parts of the public sector as inherently problematic in a democracy. At the same time, we acknowledge that

---

[4] Martinez-Vazquez and Winer (2014, chapter 1) review the literature on coercion and collective choice.

[5] The public finance classic is Musgrave's *Theory of Public Finance* (1959). The Canadian Royal Commission on Taxation (1966) is a tax reform in this tradition. There are no tax commissions based on either the political economy or exchange-contractarian traditions.

[6] *Lectures in Public Economics* by Atkinson and Stiglitz (1980) is a seminal text in the optimal tax tradition. See Salanié (2011) and Boadway (2012) for recent expositions. The Mirrlees Review (2011) is a commission based on this perspective. Boadway and Hettich debate the merits of a social planning versus a political economy approach in Winer and Shibata (2002).

while established normative public economics is often at odds with the forces of electoral competition, this does not mean that the political economy approach we explore in this Element is complete or unassailable. Indeed, in its current state, this approach lacks a widely accepted analysis of the normative properties of electoral equilibria paralleling the first theorem of welfare economics that underlies the design of public intervention in private markets.

1.1 A Brief Outline

We begin in Section 2 by discussing the centrality of competition to the study of both economics and politics. Several distinct but related ideas about the nature of political competition are presented, followed by a comparison of the elements underlying the study of economics with their counterparts in the study of politics.

The stage is then set for an evaluation of the consequences of electoral competition for the allocation of resources. We follow the three steps used in neoclassical welfare economics, beginning in Section 3 with the choice of a standard of reference appropriate for judging the efficiency of an electoral outcome. Next, we use a probabilistic voting model to develop a 'first theorem' that identifies conditions under which the equilibrium of a perfectly competitive and well functioning polity is efficient. As a complement to this analysis, we consider the implications of ignoring the fact that policy choices are part of the electoral equilibrium including difficulties that arise with identification of the redistributive effects of policy, with second-best analysis, and when the political feasibility of a proposal is not taken into account. Further discussion in an Appendix elaborates on the modelling of voter behavior, considers why an electoral equilibrium may break down because of the underlying instability of majority rule, and illustrates how determinants of electoral competitiveness can be studied.

The third step in the analogue to welfare analysis is taken in Section 4, where we use our comparison of economic and political behavior to guide the identification and discussion of significant problems that may arise with the allocations that competitive elections produce. Our discussion emphasizes the ways in which electoral competition exacerbates and attenuates these problems.

In Section 5, the evolution of tax systems, consisting of bases, rate structures, and special provisions, is explained as the outcome of sorting on economic and political margins in the face of transaction costs. The meaning of tax reform in this context is considered, and some ideas about good tax structure arising from the exchange-contractarian, social planning, and political economy approaches are compared in the light of the understanding of tax systems that we present.

In Section 6, we move from an analysis with a fixed degree of competition to one in which competitiveness is imperfect and variable. We outline various measures of competitiveness that have been proposed, illustrate the variation in competitiveness that arises in mature democracies, and sample some of the work that has explored the implications of this variation for the structure of the public finances and for economic activity. Section 7 offers a brief conclusion.

1.2 Limiting the Scope of Our Inquiry

Our analysis deals with the theory and practice of governance in liberal democracies. The use of the adjective "liberal" acknowledges the written laws and unwritten conventions that limit the extent to which any citizen may be forced to accept the consequences of government actions. These constraints on governing power significantly shape the political process, which in a liberal democracy exhibits the following characteristics: (1) each election outcome is ex ante unpredictable in the sense that everyone knows what is possible, but never what will actually occur; (2) the ex post outcome of any election is irreversible; and (3) the contest will be repeated into the foreseeable future (Przeworski 1991, chapter 1). Sartori (1976) and Bartolini (1999) see the institutions that fulfill these conditions as providing the rules of the game, and political competition as the process through which these institutions function more or less effectively.

While the authority of the state in a liberal democracy is constrained, it still encompasses a monopoly on compulsory taxation that allows a substantial reduction in the cost of transferring resources from private to public use.[7] Acquiescence to this authority goes hand-in-hand with demands from citizens who expect a substantial return on their taxes.

2 Thinking Generally about Economic and Political Competition

Although competition is an essential part of economic science, its purpose is often misconstrued in everyday conversation. There is a popular misperception that competition in a market is akin to a zero-sum game for control of resources when it is, instead, a description of how markets induce workers and owners of capital to cooperate with each other and with consumers to earn income while satisfying wants (Rubin 2019). The basic unit of analysis in economics is a voluntary transaction between two agents; competition selects the best cooperators, and the economics of a market economy is a study of cooperative

---

[7] A general monopoly on the legitimate use of force is the centerpiece of Weber's (1946, 78) definition of the state.

capitalism (Rubin's term) in which many firms and the consumers they serve can all be successful at the same time.

In contrast, politics is about conflict over control of government and the resources it commands in a situation in which only one party or coalition can be successful at any given moment. In a society where constraints on the power of the state have matured, political competition, like economic competition, may have a socially productive role – an issue we shall explore. Still, the win/lose character of election outcomes, in contrast to the sharing of the same market by different firms, imparts a zero-sum character to political rivalry that competition in markets does not have.

There is another, deeper reason why competition in politics is more about conflict than is competition in the economy. Rubin (2002, 2014) points out that from an evolutionary perspective, conflict among individuals and groups over access to resources – that is to say, politics – was more important in the development of the human brain and social behavior than was economic scarcity. This is because nature is not a strategic player, so that conflict among individuals and groups, who do act strategically, was a more potent force driving the evolution of the brain than was the struggle against nature. Thus, today we find that "when faced with an interpersonal issue that does not involve family or sex, an individual untrained in economics is more likely to treat it as a political issue than as an economic issue" (Rubin 2014, 912). Perhaps it is the study of politics rather than economics that deserves to be called the dismal science.

2.1 Approaches to the Nature of Political Competition: Objectives, Process, and Location

If we want to go beyond the general idea that political competition is the process through which democracy functions, how should we think about it? Several useful approaches have been developed, each of which points to a particular dimension of the same encompassing process:

(1) *The struggle for governing power*. This perspective defines political com-
    petition as a contest among political parties for the right to govern (e.g.,
    Schumpeter 1950; Strom 1990; Wallerstein 2004; and others). Following
    Becker (1958) and Dahl (1989), this process can be said to be fully
    competitive when the struggle for office is open to challengers and the
    electorate is broadly based. In this view, elections decide who is to choose
    public policies. They do not produce policies directly.

(2) *Responsiveness*. A competitive system is one in which parties are respon-
    sive to the demands of voters (e.g., Dahl 1971; Issacharoff and Pildes 1998;

Soroka and Wlezien 2010). The emphasis here is not on the prize sought but, rather, on how a party wins. Those who adopt this perspective measure the congruence between public opinion and the ideological platform of political parties, or estimate the responsiveness of public policies to changes in the demands of the electorate.

(3) *Preference formation and discovery.* This approach follows the previous one when we ask: What are parties are responsive to? Wohlgemuth (1995, 84, 2002), following Hayek, argues that "political competition can be reinterpreted to be ... a communication process in which preferences and opinions are created, discovered, selected and disseminated." In other words, politics is more than just a means of aggregating known preferences into a social decision. Sen (1999, chapter 6) also highlights the instrumental role of democracy in enhancing the ability of citizens to express their opinions and to support their claims to attention, a view which illustrates the close connection between political competition and ideas about democracy.

(4) *Selection and accountability.* We may also think of political competition as the process through which representatives are hired and fired. (See, e.g., Buchler 2011). Emphasis in this case is on the quality of those who compete in and win election contests. This perspective also deals with the principal–agent problem, studied extensively by Besley (2006) and others, which exists because enforcing good behavior by elected officials is costly. Popper (2013, vol. 2, 368) regards the accountability of elected representatives and the ability to replace them without bloodshed as minimal requirements for democracy, illustrating again the connection between competition and democracy.

(5) *Special-interest politics.* In this tradition, political competition is a veil for rivalry among special-interest groups. One branch of this approach, exemplified by the work of Becker (1983, 1985), emphasizes the struggle among groups to obtain favored public policies and the full cost, including excess burden, of the taxes required to pay for them. Another branch focuses on the use of resources by special interests to artificially create and capture rents (e.g., Tullock 1967; Krueger 1974).[8] In both cases, competition among groups need not always be mediated through elections (Medina 2007).

(6) *Location.* Finally, we may describe political competition in terms of its location. Competition takes place (i) in elections among candidates at a local or district level, and (ii) in elections among parties in the jurisdiction as a whole. It also takes place (iii) between elections among parties in the legislature and (iv) among governments at various levels in a federation or among countries.

---

[8] Hillman and Ursprung (2016) discuss the differences between the two branches.

These views about the nature of competition emphasize either the objectives of political parties or interest groups (1 and 5), the procedural dimensions of the competitive process (2, 3, and 4), or its location in the polity. In much of what follows, we will focus on the implications of interparty rivalry for political office while keeping the other dimensions of competition in mind. The location of competition will be of particular interest when we consider how to measure the competitiveness of elections.

2.2 A Prelude: Contrasting Elements in the Study of Economics and Politics

In Sections 3 and 4, we explore the normative character of competitive political equilibria by following the steps used in neoclassical economics to evaluate market outcomes rather than by using a social planning approach. To facilitate this analysis, it is useful to delineate beforehand the difference between the comparable elements that underlie an economic model of a market and a political economy model of public policy. Doing so will help to identify and organize discussion of the reasons why electoral equilibria are more or less likely to result in socially desirable outcomes.[9] Accordingly, we outline what we see as essential differences arising between the following pairs of basic elements, namely: (1) consumers and voters; (2) firms and political parties; and (3) markets and elections. We invite the reader to write down their own list of essential differences to compare to those we present.

2.2.1 Consumers versus Voters

Voters, like consumers, are rational, consistently fitting means to ends. But when deciding on which party to support they are less instrumental in the sense that voting is not based only on how electoral promises translate into individual economic welfare (Becker and Mulligan 2017). This reduced instrumentality has several origins, including:

(1) *Rational ignorance*: Because an individual vote has little impact on policy choice and information is costly to acquire, individuals do not find it worthwhile to acquire all of the information necessary to assess the consequences of alternative platforms (Downs 1957).[10]

---

[9] For alternative ways of proceeding, see Ursprung (1991), Glazer and Rothenberg (2001), Besley (2006, chapter 2) and Tanzi (2018).

[10] Similar logic leads to the question of why anyone bothers to vote, though in fact many do – this is the paradox of voting. Blais (2000) provides evidence for one well-used answer: voting is regarded as an act of civic duty.

(2) *Expressive voting*: Since the link between the act of voting and what governments do is weak compared to the connection between market choices and individual welfare, voting has an expressive component that is similar to the enjoyment of the solidarity that comes from cheering for a football team (Brennan and Lomasky 1993).

(3) *Ideological and other nonmarket objectives*: In political life, where it is less costly, people act in part to satisfy their loyalty to an ideology or other nonconsumption-related goals. This is not a matter of a lack of information (Caplan 2007).

(4) *Behavioral biases*: In the electoral setting, voters have a reduced incentive to deal with cognitive biases. While also present in market decision-making, the consequences are more directly costly to individuals there (e.g., Schumpeter 1950, 261–62; Frey and Stutzer 2006).[11]

As a bridge to the next pair of elements, we note that parties are surely more instrumental than are voters because parties can benefit from strategizing in the conduct of their activities.

2.2.2 Firms versus Parties

The textbook private firm continually uses its resources to produce and market goods in order to maximize the profit of its residual claimants – its shareholders. Consequently, the output of a successful firm is always in line with what its customers want and, to achieve that, the firm will follow its customers' tastes closely. In contrast, political parties have no residual claimants who bear most of the consequences of the party's success or failure (Demsetz 1982, 2008). As a result, and unlike firms, a party consists of a coalition of people with differing objectives, some of whom seek to maximize expected votes – a political analogue to profits – while others pursue ideological or policy-oriented goals even at the expense of winning (Wittman 1983; Aldrich 1995; Roemer 2001).

Like firms, parties cultivate a brand or, in political terms, an ideology, in part because this reduces information costs for its "customer base." Branding is also important in politics because it attracts the ideologically committed activists and donors who help with the problems of maintaining a political organization.

Firms and parties also differ in the credibility of their commitments. Compared to a political platform, the smaller dimensionality and greater measurability of a firm's products allows enforcement of broken promises through the courts. In cases where promises are not justiciable, the firm develops

---

[11] See also Popkin (1994), who studies how voters struggle with their (perceived) decision-making problems.

credibility by investing in a reputation for quality, an asset permitting a price premium that allows its shareholders to be favorably compensated when the firm does not cheat (Klein and Leffler 1981). The unavailability of third-party enforcement for election promises and the lack of a similar compensation mechanism make it more difficult for political parties to establish credibility in their commitment to a proposed platform, though formation of a party coalition will, to some extent, require it to honor the bargains made between coalition members (Levy 2004). An independent press in a liberal democracy may also play a role in maintaining party credibility by exposing false and broken promises, though this too will not work as surely as adjudication of a private-market contract.

2.2.3 Markets versus Elections

A market is a decentralized allocation mechanism in which relative prices channel privately owned resources toward their highest value uses. Underlying this mechanism is the fact that in a market, the transaction value of purchases and sales are closely tied – "you get what you pay for" – and consequently differences in the intensity of individual preferences play a role in shaping the equilibrium allocation. In contrast, an election is a collective choice process in which, absent unanimity, everyone must compromise and there will invariably be a difference between what each person wants for the taxes they pay and what they actually receive.

The matching of costs and benefits is made even less precise by the presence of public goods for which the levying of individual tax-prices that mimic market pricing is impractical, and by redistribution, in which case it is counterproductive, while the role of intensity of preference is further clouded by a franchise that assigns one vote to each person regardless of income and tastes.[12]

Personal agency is constrained in a collective choice process compared to a market because of the need to compromise with others. It is also reduced for a second reason. While consequential market exchange can be carried out alone, altering public policy requires cooperation within a political organization, an activity, like the provision of a public good, which is subject to problems of free riding.

---

[12] Ledyard (2006, 2014) provides an overview of the literature that deals with the problem of levying taxation according to benefits received. Vickrey (1977, 699) explains why intensity of preference is not formally incorporated in a collective choice process: "[W]hen intensity of preference is introduced ... the procedure becomes subject to subversion by the strategic misrepresentation by individuals of their true preferences, and the whole process becomes a competition in deception."

Finally, we recall that unlike the rights granted to private agents in a market, the party winning an election has the benefit of the state's monopoly on the legitimate use of force. This monopoly, which reduces the cost of financing the public sector, is constrained by the institutions of liberal democracy with more or less success in various circumstances.

3 Electoral Competition and Economic Welfare

We use the methodology of neoclassical welfare economics to study the relationship between political competition and economic welfare. Our focus is on economic efficiency, with distribution left to the political process (which does not mean that it will be ignored). There are three steps. The first is a choice of a standard of reference. The second step uses a model of a fully competitive, well-functioning polity to present a "first theorem," showing that under certain conditions, electoral equilibria will be efficient, subject to qualifications raised in step one. As a complement to this step, we consider some of the problems for policy analysis and design that arise when the fact that policy choices are part of an electoral equilibrium is ignored. The third step in the welfare analysis of electoral equilibria, which we leave for Section 4, is to inquire into the reasons why the polity may not function as well as the theorem suggests.

3.1 What Standard of Reference?

A standard of reference is required to make judgments about the quality of policies that arise as a result of electoral competition. Although we cannot offer a complete statement of such a standard, we think it must encompass the following characteristics: it should be supportable as an outcome of a fully competitive, well-functioning electoral system; and it should be cognizant of the constraints on the political process required to preserve and enhance liberal democracy.

The requirement that any Pareto superior outcome be consistent with, or supportable as, a competitive political equilibrium distinguishes our approach from public finance and normative public economics in which political institutions play no role, and where only preferences, technology (narrowly defined), and initial endowments are accepted as valid constraints on normative theorizing. Similar or related approaches to policy evaluation are used by Dixit (1996), Hettich and Winer (1999), Razin, Sadka, and Suwankiri (2011), and Acemoglu and Robinson (2013), among others.

Sen (1972) also recognizes the relevance of political context by asking whether advocated policy lies within (what he labels) the control area of government. As one example, he considers the Diamond and Mirrlees (1971a,b) theorem that an optimal tax program for redistribution requires production efficiency be preserved. The problem he points to is that the theorem assumes that any sort of commodity tax is feasible, including the taxation of all commodities with possibly very high rates on some goods. He suggests that it is appropriate to ask if, in fact, such a tax system is within the control area of government. We shall come back to this issue of political feasibility at several points.

Judgment is also required about the nature of the constraints on democratic choice that should be regarded as legitimate. For example, the inability to use market pricing for public goods and services leads to public provision of them, even if political institutions are not perfect. We accept the fact that the financing of such goods with compulsory taxation is only possible if we are willing to bear an additional or excess burden of paying for them when the necessary resources are transferred from private to public sectors.

There are other features besides the excess burden of taxation that make political institutions look inefficient when compared to their private alternatives. The reason is that there are a variety of constraints on political activity that have arisen to attenuate the principal–agent problem for citizens in a representative democracy. According to Riker (1982), Gordon (1999), Congleton (2011), and others, behind written constitutions and social conventions which protect private property and other civil and political rights lies a pluralist distribution of political power as well as the principle of countervailence, or competition among centers of power. These features of a democracy show up in part as constraints that make it impossible for the state to achieve the same allocative efficiency as a market. For example, the buying of votes through outright bribery is illegal, large contracts must go to private firms who offer the lowest price, and merit and other principles are imposed on public sector hiring and firing. There are rules forcing executives to seek approval from the legislature to spend tax revenue (Cox and Weingast 2018), veto points that make redeployment of public resources difficult are built into many legislative systems (Tsebelis 2002), and other constraints on legislative decision-making may become entrenched because they help to ensure that durable political bargains in legislatures can be made despite the potential instability of majority rule (Weingast and Marshall 1988). As a consequence, the policy instruments that can be used to redistribute resources toward favored supporters are imprecise and hence more costly, with spillovers extending beyond party supporters that further increase the social cost of the democracy (Hartle 1993).

These features of a well-functioning democracy – the technology of the public sector, like the technology underlying private market activity – are the net result of multiple prior decisions made by the community. As such, they both incentivize and restrict the policies that can be chosen under existing rules. The argument implicit in a social planning approach to normative public economics is that all such political constraints should be ignored because it is technically feasible to produce a different outcome that is more highly valued. From our perspective, this is analogous to arguing that a better output mix would arise in private markets if there were no market constraints on private activity. It begs the question of which particular constraints might be ignored, and which are essential to the operation of a liberal democracy.

A social planning counter to this argument is that political constraints are different because individual preferences underlying voting behavior and constraints arising from the operation of political institutions may be changed by providing information and/or by persuasion, thus producing better policy choices. However, whether information, paternalism, or coercion can legitimately be used to alter what is currently a constraint on allocative outcomes is a general problem not specific to collective choice settings. Moreover, if it is believed that a policy can be improved upon because of its origin in misinformation, is it not preferable to deal directly with the source of misinformation rather than to advocate a change in policy on the basis of a belief that this is what voters would have wished?

3.2 A First Theorem for Competitive Political Economies

If voting by each citizen is deterministic and preferences are common know-ledge, it has been known since the work of Condorcet (1785) that majority rule can lead to cycling over the alternatives considered. When preferences are known with certainty, the existence of an equilibrium under pure majority rule requires restrictions on the dimensionality of the issue space and on preferences. In the famous median voter model of Black (1958), there is only a single dimension over which each voter's (indirect) preferences are single peaked. In that case, the outcome corresponding to the median of the ideal points of the voters is a Condorcet winner – a proposal that cannot lose to any alternative in a pair-wise sequence of majority-rule votes.[13]

When Black's framework is used to model redistribution through the fiscal system by means of equal lump sum transfers financed by a proportional income tax, Meltzer and Richard (1981, 1983) show that the net benefit for the median or decisive voter rises with skewness in the distribution of income as measured by the ratio of mean to median income.[14] That ratio also serves as an indicator of the

---

[13] Palfrey (1984) extends the model to allow for entry, which forces existing parties to move away from the median to prevent undercutting by new entrants.

[14] This model stimulated a literature on the political economy of income taxation including Roberts (1977), Snyder and Kramer (1988), and Berliant and Gouveia (2021), among others. See also Romer (1975).

associated excess burden of taxation because the median voter balances the fiscal net benefit he or she receives with its distortionary cost (Hsu and Yang 2008).

This median voter outcome, while stable, is not socially efficient unless the distribution of preferences around the median is symmetric so that those who want more public services are "balanced" with those who want less (Bowen 1943). Vote trading in a legislature after an election may lead to an improvement in an "unbalanced" situation, although this usually works well only for those who end up in the majority (Tullock 1959).

Adding to the space of public policies so that governments can discriminate more effectively is another way that everyone's welfare might be improved (Wittman 1995, 153). But adding complexity also brings back the instability of majority rule if preferences are common knowledge. For example, if the distribution of the tax burden as well as government size is being decided upon in an election, for any proposal about the distribution of after-tax incomes made by one party, there will always be another that can be offered by some other party that will attract more votes. This means that total votes for any party will be a discontinuous function of its available policy choices, making it unlikely that a Nash electoral equilibrium will exist. Moreover, in such circumstances, and absent a Condorcet winner, a sequence of elections may lead anywhere in the issue space, including points outside of the Pareto set of those voting (McKelvey 1976).

Acknowledging that parties have only probabilistic knowledge about voting behavior provides a way out of both instability and inefficiency. Probabilistic knowledge of preferences, which is characteristic of what party strategists possess, converts intensity of individual preferences into a probability of electoral support for each party, which is a continuous function of its policy platform. In this way intensity of preference, which the one person one vote rule attenuates in a deterministic voting setting, is brought back into the electoral process. At the same time, the probabilistic nature of voting removes the discontinuities in the total votes for a party that make the search for an electoral equilibrium difficult. A Nash electoral equilibrium in pure strategies may then arise even when the issue space is multidimensional, provided each party's objective, which we assume in what follows is its expected vote, is globally concave as well as continuous in its platform.[15] Equilibrium exists even though voters (still) make a discrete choice about which party to support.[16] In this electoral system, there may be an invisible hand in the electoral process.

---

[15] Work on probabilistic voting includes Coughlin (1992, 2015), Lindbeck and Weibull (1987), Enelow and Hinich (1989), Chen (2000), and Adams, Merrill, and Grofman (2005). Alternative approaches are discussed by Wallerstein (2004) and Austen-Smith (2008).

[16] Voters may also be unsure of what governments will do. This is not essential for an equilibrium but will become interesting when we consider problems with political equilibria.

3.2.1 A Representation Theorem

A probabilistic spatial voting model may have an equilibrium that can be represented by the optimization of a political support function that corresponds to a social welfare function even though no active social planning is involved, a result first shown by Coughlin and Nitzan (1981).[17] We shall refer to this result as a representation theorem. Presentation of such a framework is the second step of our welfare analysis.

The particular spatial voting model that we adopt for this analysis is significantly simplified. Constraints on collective choice that are part of the standard of reference are only implicit in the model (analogously, transactions costs are only implicit in the canonical model of perfect competition in a market). The set of policy instruments from which parties fashion their platforms is assumed known, fixed, and well-behaved, as are the parties and candidates.[18] Finally, we note that the set of issues decided by any election is big, perhaps too big for the long-run stability of democratic institutions, including complete determination of the distribution of individual welfare.

The demonstration in this section that under certain conditions electoral competition may result in an economically efficient allocation of resources is more mathematical in nature than are arguments in the Element as a whole. Readers less interested in mathematical detail may wish to read the text for a general sense of the argument, and then turn to the discussion following in which some of the implications of treating policy choices as part of a competitive political equilibrium are drawn out.

Our setting is an electoral contest between two parties, each of which chooses its platform to maximize the total vote they can expect to receive in the next election.[19] Voters know who they will support – the party that promises them the highest utility – and everyone votes sincerely. But parties have only probabilistic (common) knowledge of how the voters will behave.

An incumbent party i and an opposition party o compete by offering and delivering a multidimensional policy platform or program s^p, $p = \{i, o\}$, (e.g., a vector of tax rates, tax bases, special provisions, and public expenditures and transfers) to an electorate of J voters with indirect utility functions $v_j(s)$. Usually the number of instruments in these programs will be much less than the number

---

[17] Ledyard (1984) provides a related approach in which the act of voting is a costly activity. See also Coughlin's (1992) later exposition.

[18] On agenda control and other aspects of political manipulation, which we mostly leave in the background, see especially Riker (1986, 1990). Candidate selection is considered by Besley (2006), Galasso and Nannicini (2011), Buchler (2011), and many others referenced in these works.

[19] The multiparty case is considered by Wittman (1987), Lin, Enelow, and Dorussen (1999), and Schofield (2007).

of voters. (This structure is discussed in the Section 5). Voters cast their ballots sincerely for the party that promises them a higher utility, so the probability a voter will support the incumbent is

$$\pi_j^i = \begin{cases} 1 & \text{if } v_j(s^i) - v_j(s^o) > 0 \\ 0 & \text{otherwise.} \end{cases} \tag{3.1}$$

But we suppose that, *as seen by the parties,* the probability a citizen votes for the incumbent is known by both parties to be described by a density function f, which is increasing in the difference in the utilities the voter derives from each platform:

$$f_j\Big(v_j(s^i) - v_j(s^o)\Big); \; \partial f_j/\partial (v_j^i - v_j^o) > 0. \tag{3.2}$$

To fashion a competitive policy platform, the incumbent chooses a platform that maximizes its expected vote EV_i given the platform of its challenger, subject to the structure of the economy which we write generally as $R(s)=0$:

$$Max_{\{s^i\}} \; EV_i = \Sigma_j^J \; f_j\Big(v_j(s^i) - v_j(s^o)\Big) \text{ subject to } R(s) = 0 \tag{3.3}$$

If everyone votes, $EV_o = J - EV_i$.[20] In that case the solution to the opposition's problem is equivalent to that of the incumbent and party platforms will be identical in the electoral equilibrium if one exists. (Divergence of platforms can be introduced if first order conditions for the optimal policy platforms for each party are not the same for some reason.)

If each party's expected vote is globally concave over the issue space as well as continuous in s, so that there is a positive probability, no matter how small, of each voter supporting either party, a Nash equilibrium in pure strategies in this contest will exist. If the concavity of EV is strict, the equilibrium will be unique. Further discussion of the conditions underlying the existence of an equilibrium along with a demonstration of how the model can be adapted to expose determinants of the degree of electoral competition are provided in the Appendix.

For a policy set $s = \{s_l, l = 1, 2, \ldots, L\}$, each element of which may in general affect many different voters, the equilibrium platform is defined by the following first order conditions where party subscripts are dropped because platforms converge, and λ is the Lagrange multiplier on the constraint:

---

[20] Roemer (2001) specifies expected vote functions directly, thus allowing for correlations between individual voting decisions assumed away in (3.3).

$$\sum_{j}^{J} \frac{\partial f_j}{\partial v_j} \cdot \frac{\partial v_j}{\partial s_l} + \lambda \cdot \frac{\partial R}{\partial s_l} = 0; \; l = 1, 2, \ldots, L \qquad (3.4)$$

The representation theorem is essentially the observation that the competitive equilibrium just described can be represented by the maximization of a synthetic political support function subject to the same constraint(s) facing the parties. As a proof, it is sufficient to show that the equilibrium can be replicated by the constrained optimization of a (political support) function S that is a weighted sum of voter utilities. Assuming that S is concave in s after substitution of the constraint, the problem that can be used to replicate the Nash equilibrium is:

$$Max_{\{s\}} \; S(s) = \Sigma_j^J \; \theta_j \cdot v_j(s) \text{ subject to } R(s) = 0, \qquad (3.5)$$

where $\theta_j = \partial f_j / \partial v_j$, the sensitivity of each voter to a change in their welfare evaluated at the Nash equilibrium. These influence weights are particular numbers, one for each voter. This problem can be used to represent the Nash electoral outcome because the first order conditions for its solution are exactly those in (3.4) defining each party's politically optimal policy choices in the equilibrium.

It is important to recognize that the support function S in (3.5) is not a social welfare function since the weights determining the relative importance of individuals in the equilibrium are determined by the interplay of contesting parties and not on the basis of some normative theory.

Other forms of the support function will arise depending on the nature of the density function describing voting behavior. For example, Coughlin and Nitzan and Coughlin (1992, chp4) show that if the probability of voting has the Luce form, depending on a ratio of utilities, the support function that is optimized in an equilibrium is a weighted sum of the logs of utilities. In each case, since a weighted sum of utilities is maximized, it follows that equilibrium policy choices are Pareto efficient while being situated along the Pareto frontier at a point that takes the weights into account. In this probabilistic voting framework, there is an invisible hand in the political process.

We can compare political decision-making in the spatial voting framework we are describing to the use of the Hicks–Kaldor criterion in benefit–cost analysis. Here voting converts ordinal, noncomparable preference rankings into cardinal, interpersonally comparable numbers – a probability of voting for each party – allowing the interests of different voters to be traded off. But unlike most benefit–cost analyses, 'distributional' weights from the equilibrium are applied to each citizen's welfare. Moreover, the outcome may also depend on how voters view the social implications of their situation, a factor that benefit–cost analysis does not consider.

As an example of the use of the theorem, suppose s consists of a large set of tax rates t_j, one for each voter, levied on some base in order to finance a public good G. For convenience, we also assume each tax instrument only affects the welfare of the taxpayer indicated. If total revenue is $R(t_1, \ t_2, \ldots, t_J, G)$ the first order conditions, analogous to (3.4), characterizing the equilibrium fiscal structure are:

$$\frac{\theta_j \cdot \frac{\partial v_j}{\partial t_j}}{\frac{\partial R}{\partial t_j}} = -\lambda, \qquad j = 1, 2, \ldots, J, \tag{3.6}$$

and

$$\sum_j \theta_j \cdot \frac{\partial v_j}{\partial G} = \lambda \left(1 - \frac{\partial R}{\partial G} \right), \tag{3.7}$$

where λ is the Lagrange multiplier associated with the government budget constraint $R(t_1, \ t_2, \ldots, t_J, G) = G$.[21] In this equilibrium, platforms are chosen so as to equalize the marginal political cost or loss of support per dollar of revenue raised across tax instruments, and each of these are in turn set equal to the marginal political benefit of another dollar of public spending net of the effects of any additional tax revenue that arises when G is increased.[22] Here a voter's political sensitivity to a change in their welfare, indexed by θ_j, determines how well they are treated in the equilibrium. As (3.6) indicates, if marginal utility diminishes, a relatively influential or sensitive voter will be taxed less heavily. We should also note that in this equilibrium, there will never be an exact matching for any citizen of the taxes they pay and benefits they would like to receive in exchange.

3.2.2 Some Implications of an Equilibrium Framework for Policy Analysis

Before turning to an analysis of why outcomes often differ from those described by this fully competitive, well-functioning political system, we explore some of the implications for policy analysis that arise when public policy is regarded as part of an electoral equilibrium.

---

[21] Here $v_j = v_j(t_j, G)$. The presence of G in the revenue function allows for complementarity between the public good and the tax base.

[22] For a computable version of a similar model calibrated to US data, see Rutherford and Winer in Hettich and Winer (1999, chapter 7). A synthetically calibrated version is used by Warskett, Winer, and Hettich to explore the income/consumption tax mix use: see the appendix to Winer (2019).

Efficient Redistribution and the Identification of Inefficient Policies

We should expect redistribution toward poorer voters in the equilibrium described by the spatial voting model. The prospect of losing office induces parties who want to continue to govern to cater to all sorts of voters by never moving too far toward their own party's most preferred choices at the expense of minority interests, including the poor whose opposition mounts as they are increasingly ignored in favor of other groups.[23]

This redistribution will be conducted as efficiently as possible in the well-functioning electoral system. This is evident from condition (3.6) when all of the influence weights (the θ_j) are assumed to be equal. In that case, the equilibrium tax system is one in which tax instruments are chosen so that their marginal welfare costs per unit of revenue are equalized, thus minimizing the total welfare cost of financing a public sector of given size.[24] More generally, if political influence is distributed unequally, unweighted marginal welfare losses for different tax sources may vary significantly as parties trade off the welfare of, and support from, distinct groups of voters, even though the equilibrium lies on the Pareto utility frontier.

This discussion points to a problem of distinguishing between redistribution and inefficient tax design. In a well-functioning electoral system with unequal influence weights, a standard analysis that detects faults in tax design by looking for inequalities in unweighted welfare costs across tax instruments will associate *all* of the observed inequalities with bad tax design, even though competition between parties fully incorporates all relevant welfare losses. We do not have to think that actual political equilibria are fully efficient to agree that some parts of the inequalities in unweighted welfare costs are due to redistribution that is being conducted at minimal cost in the pursuit of electoral support. But which parts?

A Challenge for Second-Best Analysis

Another interesting problem that arises in an equilibrium framework concerns second-best analysis.

As Boadway (2017, 260) writes "the second-best problem aris[es] either from immutable distortions in a subset of markets or from limitations in the policy

---

[23] Why then do we see a rise in inequality in mature democracies over the past few decades? Erikson (2015) points to the poor who do not vote. Scheve and Stasavage (2017) point to the fact that societies are divided along other cleavages besides wealth (see also Roemer 1998), beliefs about what is fair (see also Sheffrin 2013), and, like Erikson, to the success of richer voters in slowing policy responses. The relative importance of the factors listed is not known.

[24] For a restatement in terms of marginal excess burdens and marginal efficiency costs, see Winer and Hettich (1998, 382).

instruments available to government." In such circumstances policies designed to minimize the distortion in just one sector of the economy cannot be relied upon to improve welfare because of distortions existing elsewhere. The McKee-West (1981) criticism of the second-best, however, challenges the existence of the initial condition by arguing that the initial distortion or constraint on a policy instrument is the outcome of prior optimization that resulted in a competitive political equilibrium.

Consider, for example, a government subsidy – the second-best instrument in this case – given to a monopolist's competitor in the same or in a closely related sector in order to minimize the distortion between price and marginal cost in the monopolist's choices, thereby offsetting the consequences of the monopoly for economic welfare. The McKee-West argument is that the second distortion, due to the subsidy, is unlikely to increase efficiency overall. The reason is that the granting of the initial monopoly represents the equilibrium solution to a prior political choice and, as such, reflects a first-best solution given the operation of a political process in which production inefficiency is one of many costs of allocating property rights. Hence if policy is used to "undo" the advantage conferred by that political process it is undoing an equilibrium, and under the pressure of electoral competition it will illicit further reaction to restore at least some of the advantage originally conferred. Moreover, the adjustments arising elsewhere in the economy in response to this "improvement" would represent movements away from a previously optimal solution.

Do information problems facing governments constitute a special case? Tax structures may be chosen in part to overcome incentive compatibility constraints arising from asymmetric information concerning the ability of individuals to lower their tax liabilities. These are second-best policies if the source of the asymmetry is assumed to be out of reach of the policy maker. It should be noted, however, that the mechanisms the government is allowed to use to acquire information derive from a political equilibrium in which the community has decided how much coercive power is permissible. The McKee-West critique applied in this situation suggests that policies to get around the asymmetric information problem may challenge the implied social contract concerning knowledge and control of private behavior. This is another issue that deserves further consideration.

Political Feasibility in Policy Design and Advocacy

Even when it is accepted that alternative policy designs can produce superior outcomes, advisors recognize that a proposal must be supportable as a political equilibrium – that is, politically feasible – or it will not be adopted. As we noted earlier, social planning explicitly refrains from such a consideration. Feasibility is an issue of longstanding concern in the public administration literature (e.g., Dror 1969; Meltsner 1972). Dror argues that the infeasibility of an alternative should sometimes be taken as a challenge rather than accepted as a constraint, though it is not clear when one ought to do so. It is less common to see feasibility considered in the public economics literature, though it does arise from time to time; see Besley and Coate (2003), Acemoglu, Golosov and Tsyvinski (2008), Acemoglu and Robinson (2013), Oh (2017), Bierbrauer, Boyer and Peichl (2020), and Kangas (2021).[25] The issue is given further attention in section 3.2.3. Here we use examples to illustrate a general problem of policy design that may arise when political feasibility is ignored.

As deputy assistant secretary of the Treasury from 1983 to 1985, Charles McLure directed a team charged with drawing up a US tax reform known as Treasury I (1984). This document proposed a broad base federal income tax for the United States, despite economic theory that at the time had swung in favor of an expenditure tax. The rationale for the Treasury proposal, according to the account in McLure and Zodrow (2007), was that the designers in the Treasury knew that one component of the expenditure tax would never be accepted by the president and, as a result, the outcome would be worse than if the Treasury proposed a broad-based income tax. The component they were sure would be missing was the taxation of inheritances and bequests, which is required to preserve tax equity when an expenditure tax replaces a personal income tax

A second example involves the Mirrlees Review's (2011) advocacy of reduced corporate taxation. In the review, capital income is more heavily sheltered from direct taxation and inheritance taxes are advocated as a means of maintaining overall tax progressivity.[26] Inheritance taxes are also recommended as a way to improve equality of opportunity. The problem facing those who want to put more emphasis on wealth transfer taxation is that this form of taxation has been declining in most Western countries for several decades, perhaps because of opposition from aging electorates that want to pass on hard-earned wealth to their children, perhaps because of successful lobbying by monied interests.[27] Whatever the reason, if the decline in wealth transfer taxation is regarded as a constraint to be factored into tax design, the proposals in the Mirrlees Review might look somewhat different. A Nordic style dual

---

[25] For example, Bierbrauer and colleagues (2020) suggest a way of predicting what sort of income tax changes are politically feasible.

[26] See also Boadway, Chamberlain, and Emmerson (2010).

[27] Profeta, Scambrosetti, and Winer (2014) review patterns of wealth transfer taxation in G7 countries and evaluate the aging hypothesis. The decline of estate taxation in the United States is examined by Graetz and Shapiro (2005).

income tax that involves taxation of capital income at a rate lower than labor income could be a preferred alternative.

In both cases, the advocacy of a multipart social plan was likely to result in only part of the overall proposal being accepted, producing an outcome that is no longer optimal when judged from the original standpoint. This is an important point.

3.2.3 Political Feasibility, Tectonic Policies and Schumpeterian Competition

It is worthwhile to explore the nature of political feasibility somewhat further. We do so here in a manner that leads to introduction of a form of political competition that we have not so far identified.[28]

Suppose we consider a proposed policy in period 1, s_1, that will affect individual welfare both now $\left(v_j^1\right)$ and in the future $\left(v_j^2\right)$. Suppose also that the policy implemented in period 1 might, by changing the distribution of income or other factors, also change the political weight of some individuals or groups in a second period. Then (leaving discounting and any constraints imposed by the structure of the economy aside), given the support function

$$S(s_1) = \sum_j \theta_j v_j^1(s_1) + \sum_j \theta_j(s_1) v_j^2(s_1), \tag{3.8}$$

the governing party competing for support would adopt s_1 only if

$$\frac{dS}{ds_1} = \sum_j \theta_j \frac{dv_j^1}{ds_1} + \sum_j \left[\frac{d\theta_j(s_1)}{ds_1} v_j^2 + \theta_j \frac{dv_j^2}{ds_1} \right] > 0. \tag{3.9}$$

This is a minimal condition for the political feasibility of the policy. An ideal policy will make S as high as possible.

The decision made will differ from the advice given by a benefit–cost analyst (who avoids politics) for at least two reasons. This analyst would not consider either the heterogeneity of political influence, nor the impact of the policy on the political equilibrium. That is, the benefit–cost analyst considers whether or not

$$\frac{dS}{ds_1} = \sum_j \frac{dv_j^1}{ds_1} + \sum_j \frac{dv_j^2}{ds_1} > 0. \tag{3.10}$$

Attempts have been made to incorporate normatively defined versions of the θ_j into benefit–cost studies (see Boardman et al. 2020 for a discussion). But most such studies weight gains and losses across individuals equally. Induced changes in the θ_j are simply ignored. The political strategist will be interested in the economist's

---

[28] This discussion of feasibility builds on a framework suggested by Acemoglu and Robinson (2013).

evaluation of the economic consequences of policy choices – the terms in dv_j^k/ds_1 – and will fill in their own estimates of the θ_j and of the $d\theta_j(s_1)/ds_1$ indicating how the adoption of the policy alters current and future support.

The feasibility of policies will evolve over time as political influence does. Demographic aging, for example, will alter the relative influence of young and old and hence change the political profitability attached to social welfare programs directed at these groups (Profeta 2002), perhaps leading to the crowding out of social spending as the pension demands of an aging electorate rise (Lindert 2019).

Sometimes policy is designed to pro-actively alter future political behavior. For example, the policy of Margaret Thatcher, when prime minister of the United Kingdom, of selling public housing to their occupants was surely intended to change the voting behavior of new homeowners in a Conservative direction. Immigration policy is another strategy that may be used to shift the distributions of electoral support (Razin, Sadka, and Suwankiri 2011). We might think of the European Union as a long-term project aimed at creating shifts in attitudes toward political integration across member states. These are all examples of what Young (1991) refers to as tectonic policy, which he thought of as yet another dimension of electoral competition, one that is analogous to Schumpeterian creative destruction in a market.

4 What Can Go Wrong?

The identification and analysis of problems with resource allocation through democratic politics is the third and last step in the neoclassical approach to normative political economy. We use our enumeration of the differences between economic and political behavior as a guide in order to focus on the problems that we think are among the most important for economic wellbeing.[29] In so doing, we pay attention to the role of competition and political institutions in exacerbating and attenuating them. The standard of reference lying behind this discussion is provided by the perfectly competitive, well-functioning polity described in the previous section.

The general implication of admitting such problems into our understanding of the competitive political system is that observed policy choices are complex mixtures of "good" and "bad" elements.

4.1 Problems Due to the Behavior of Voters

Falling victim to false advertising and adopting beliefs not in accordance with the facts have adverse consequences for consumers that are relatively easy to

---

[29] There are no empirically based rankings of these problems.

observe in a market. Consequently, market competition forces the dissembling firm to bear the cost of providing false information and gives incentives to its rivals to expose false beliefs. However, in politics, as many authors have observed, such problems may persist even when competition is intense.

Suppose a voter's probability of voting is $f_j(v_j(s^i) - v_j(s^o), C(s^i, s^o))$. Here C is a proxy for costly political advertising and related activities which, we assume, have an influence on voting behavior independently of their consequences for individual welfare. This could involve manipulation of biases in personal decision-making (Jones and Baumgartner 2005), false signals about party platforms, or false information about the voter's economic and social situation (Grossman and Helpman 2019).

In this case, the synthetic problem that can be used to replicate politically optimal policies in the electoral equilibrium is now different from that in (3.5). It becomes

$$\text{Max}_{\{s\}}\ S(s) = \Sigma_j\{\theta_j.\ v_j(s) + \theta_j^C.\ C(s)\} \text{ subject to } R(s) = 0 \tag{4.1}$$

where $\theta_j^C = \partial f_j/\partial C$ at the equilibrium.[30]

Public policy no longer leads to a socially efficient outcome, as the welfare of voters is traded off for resources used for influencing voting behavior in other ways. (This problem is in addition to one that arises if some people avoid the truth, presenting strange beliefs to parties competing for their vote, as in Caplan (2007). In that case, electoral outcomes may to some extent be based on a false vision of the world even if $C = 0$).

If C enters the indirect utility function of voters only because it reduces their net cost of information, the situation reverts to the efficient result summarized by (3.5). The difficulty of distinguishing between these two cases may serve as a foundation for campaign finance laws that equalize resources among contending parties while limiting the overall amount of money in electoral contests.

The question to ask at this point is whether electoral competition helps to reveal the price that voters must pay for satisfaction of their demands. Downs (1957) and Hinich and Munger (1994) explain why parties compete with each other on the basis of general attitudes, or ideology, toward economic and social affairs, because this allows them to simplify their brand for the voting public.[31] Still, the nature of the goods supplied publicly make the information problem for voters more complex than in the private sector, especially when experience

---

[30] Grossman and Helpman (2001) use this kind of support function in their analysis of special-interest politics.

[31] As an example, we note that Poole and Rosenthal (1997) have demonstrated that just two dimensions are needed to explain role call voting in the US Congress.

goods are involved: compare, for example, competition for personal deodorants in the private sector with voter adjudication of competing promises concerning public health care. Moreover, unlike a court of law where speech is highly regulated, the rules required to protect freedom of speech in a democracy make the detection of fake news and false advertising difficult.

Nyhan (2020, 232) reminds us that "false information, misperceptions and conspiracy theories are general features of human society." The rise of social media has made the information and decision-making issues seem even more meaningful. The changing forms and decline in the relative cost of information of all types has led to doubts that the Internet has made the electorate better informed or more capable of making decisions. People who believe that Covid vaccines are used to inject computer chips, or that the world is threatened by a cabal of Jewish bankers and pedophiles, can now find a community of like minds online. Moreover, surveillance capitalism (Zuboff 2019), based on the processing of enormous amounts of data from personal Internet use, will surely be used by political strategists to try and bend individual voting behavior.

Statistical evidence on these matters is only recently arriving and is still ambiguous. In their survey of Internet use, del Vicario and colleagues (2016, 558) find using Facebook data that users tend to aggregate in communities of interest, which fosters confirmation bias and polarization. This comes at the expense of the quality of the information and leads to proliferation of narratives fomented by mistrust. On the other hand, Boxell, Gentzkow, and Shapiro (2020) look at trends in political polarization across nine OECD countries and find no correlation between Internet penetration and polarization. Theocharis and Lowe (2016) randomly assigned access to social media platforms and measured how the use of these tools affected levels of civic engagement. Although political knowledge is measured here only indirectly, the effects of exposure to information are small. In a study directed at the 2016 US presidential election, Allcott and Gentzkow (2017) found that even if fake news stories circulated widely on social media, the average American saw, at most, several of them.

A consensus on the significance of misinformation for voters and policy outcomes remains elusive. As Tucker and colleagues (2018, 15) conclude, "[a]lthough there is ... agreement regarding the high prevalence of misinformation and propaganda in online platforms, whether or not it has any impact on ... levels of political knowledge, trust in democratic institutions, or political polarization remains an open question."

As we noted, work that bears on the questions of what voters know and how they decide is ongoing. We cannot review it comprehensively here but offer instead a few intriguing examples. Alesina, Favero, and Giavazzi (2019) show that austerity based on spending cuts in sixteen advanced economies resulted in smaller output losses compared to policies based on tax increases. They suggest that this counterintuitive finding may be explained by the greater removal of uncertainty about future tax raises engineered by expenditure cuts relative to tax increases that leave entitlement programs intact (4–5). Rueda and Stegmueller (2019, 223) argue that their extensive evidence concerning the nature of redistributive preferences supports the view that "an increase in expected income decreases the probability to vote for a Left or redistributive party in Western Europe and in the United States." These explanations are based on an understanding of individual behavior in which instrumental foresight plays a significant role.

The findings of Stimson and Wager (2020) on issues that involve the economy, political contests, and science indicate that long-term trends in beliefs tend to converge slowly toward the evidence provided that the issues involved are controversial. As they say, "a good brawl produces a more informed public." (68). In the end, however, Stimson and Wager are less hopeful about what people know, pointing to the paucity of vigorous public debates.[32]

Given the difficulties citizens have knowing what policies are best for themselves, it is reasonable to ask if the inefficiency involved when people do not vote their true interests, somehow defined, can be used as a basis for advocating policy guided by benefit–cost analysis? Sunstein (2013, 235–6), recognizing that politicians and interest groups try to manipulate voters by enlisting cognitive biases, argues that people's inability to properly assess risk provides a rationale for contrary government actions, which may even be desired by citizens who know they have difficulty in such circumstances.[33] He suggests, as do Flyvbjerg and Bester (2021), that decision-making by benefit–cost analysis at least ought to be an ingredient in the democratic process.

The question of whether and when we should defer to experts is a long standing one. Wiseman (1989, 181–2) concludes that "If they [the experts] can persuade others that is in their interest to cede authority over particular matters, subject to constraints decided by those others, then no insurmountable difficulty arises." Frey and Stutzer (2006) argue that especially when there are cognitive biases, public discussion, an essential component of democracy, helps

---

[32] We should also recognize that even if citizens make decisions well, that does not guarantee that all private information they accumulate will be used effectively in determining a collective choice outcome, as in private market, since heterogeneity of, and uncertainty about, voters' preferences can block information aggregation (Feddersen and Pessendorfer 1997; Austen-Smith and Feddersen 2009; Mandeler 2012).

[33] See also Sunstein (2018, 2020).

citizens to learn about their own biases. Frey and Stutzer's conclusion, however, complementing that of the Hewlet Foundation, is that whether the democratic process leads to policies that correct people's biases, or instead helps special interests to harvest rents, is not a settled matter.

4.2 Problems Due to the Nature of Political Parties

Earlier we pointed out that a political party does not have a residual claimant who can consistently benefit from the value generated by always carrying through with its election promises, nor are broken promises justiciable in a court of law. As a result, while the preferences of voters extend into the future, a sequence of political equilibria may not bridge the present and the future very well (Kydland and Prescott 1977).

The archetypical application to the public sector concerns taxation of investment by a multinational firm (e.g., Fischer 1980). Politically optimal tax policy from the perspective of a first "period" will consider the feedback of tax policy in a second period on policy outcomes in both periods. However, once the second period arrives, the governing party will be tempted to change its previously announced policy and expropriate investments that, in the second period, are now irreversible. This change in previously announced policy can be anticipated by investors, eventually leading to them go elsewhere.

To further expose this argument, consider the simplified two period support function $S = S_1(w_1(t_1, t_2)) + S_2(w_2(t_1, t_2))$, where any political discount factor is ignored, policy is just a single tax rate for each period, and the consequences of policy for the welfare of voters is summarized in each period by a function w. The role of t_2 in w_1 reflects the importance of expectations of investors in their decision-making. The problem in this context is that in period two, the governing party has two choices.[34] It can continue with the "ex ante optimization" decision made in period 1 that recognized how the promise to fix future taxes would affect investors' expectations represented by $(\partial w_1)/(\partial t_2)$, that is, where t_2 was chosen to satisfy:

$$\frac{\partial S_2}{\partial w_2}\frac{\partial w_2}{\partial t_2} + \frac{\partial S_1}{\partial w_1}\frac{\partial w_1}{\partial t_2} + \lambda\frac{\partial R}{\partial t_2} = 0, \tag{4.2}$$

in which the consequences for the budget are summarized by the constraint $R(t_1, t_2, w_1, w_2) = 0$. Or it can choose "ex post optimization," taking both t_1 and w_1 as given in period two, choosing t_2 so as to enjoy an extra levy on capital that is now fixed in place and that can be used to benefit its supporters. In this case, optimization involves promising the t_2 from (4.2) in period 1 and then setting a

---

[34] This exposition is suggested by Bénassy-Quéré and colleagues (2010, 89)

new t_2 in period 2 defined by (4.2) with $\partial w_1 / \partial t_2$ set equal to zero. (The consequences for the budget restraint summarized by $\partial R / \partial t_2$ will also differ in the two cases.)

The two choices facing the government are the same only if expectations by investors are unimportant in their decisions. Otherwise, the government will be tempted to renege on its promises to investors despite the adverse consequences for investment over the longer run that follow. A more general conclusion in the context of a discussion of taxation according to tax elasticities is that governments that cannot commit tend to neglect the longer run elasticity of their bases, and so tax bases with relatively greater long run elasticity too highly. As Fischer (1980, 104) points out, for these adverse consequences to occur, the expectations of investors and, we add, of taxpayers generally, need not be fully rational so long as they depend in some way on announcements about future policy.

Similar problems arise with other policies where expectations are involved and decisions cannot be easily reversed, such as decisions about the openness of markets to international competition (Fernandez and Rodrik 1991; Bardhan and Yang 2004). The underlying problem is the difficulty for groups of citizens who are likely to win from more open markets to make binding, politically sanctioned side deals with those who are likely to lose (Acemoglu 2003).

What is the role of electoral competition in the time inconsistency problem? It both exacerbates and attenuates it. It is electoral rivalry that pushes the incumbent to renege on its promises in the hope of profiting from its dissembling. But competition for electoral support may also attenuate the problem in at least two ways: through competition to attract contributions from lobbyists and activists, and because of opposition from potential losers.

Suppose there is lobbying by investors with payoffs to parties $C_1(t_1, t_2)$ and $C_2(t_1, t_2)$. These C' s may arise for reasons discussed previously where it was possible to use resources to influence voting behavior even if this is not in the best interests of the voters. Incorporating contributions, the support function becomes $S' = \{S + C_1 + C_2\}$ and the time consistent solution with $\partial w_1 / \partial t_2 \neq 0$ may now become feasible because in the second period the governing party will take the negative effect that raising t_2 will have on C_2 into account in setting t_1 and t_2. It may still pay the government to expropriate and give up all C_2, but there is now a punishment for doing so. The consistent policy, if it emerges, will not be as good for voters as when $C_1 + C_2 = 0$. But if these contributions lead to enforcement of the initial promise about t_2, the overall result will be better than it would be if expropriation is seen by investors as the government's likely strategy. Marceau and Smart (2003) reach a similar conclusion.

A second channel by which competition among agents can attenuate time inconsistency utilizes the feedback effect of lost investment on future wages and employment. Let $\partial w_2/\partial t_2 < 0$ now also reflect the wage and job losses for noninvestor citizens in period two arising from foregone investment. By advertising these consequences of expropriation to citizens who vote retrospectively on the government's performance, competing parties can impose on the incumbent an additional political cost, lowering the value of expropriation relative to the time consistent solution.[35] Bates and Lien (1985) explain how firms can contribute to this pressure through the threat of migration even in the absence of political contributions.

In this sort of situation, a more general mechanism may be at work. Welfare losses mean that voters suffering them go into the future with reduced utility and, given diminishing marginal utility, with an increased willingness to demand compensatory action in subsequent elections to prevent serious deterioration in their lifetime welfare (Howitt 1990).[36] Such reasoning also leads Aidt and Magris (2006) to conclude that as long as parties care about the future and voters care about their performance, time-consistent policies can survive in an electoral equilibrium.

Institutional arrangements may further reduce the scale of the problem. It has been widely argued that a monetary rule implemented by an independent central bank avoids a high-inflation equilibrium arising from the government's repeated attempts to use expansionary monetary policy to increase employment by trying (and ultimately failing) to take advantage of money wage contracts that have been agreed to prior to the change in monetary policy. Such an institutional arrangement that replaces discretionary, time-inconsistent policy actions has been adopted by many countries since the Kydland and Prescott paper first appeared. This is one area where normative ideas about public policy have clearly gravitated to an institutional level.[37]

With independent central banking and inflation targeting widely observed, the question arises as to why do we not observe "central taxing"?[38] One possible answer is that it is hard to write a contract with a central taxer that will specify all the many dimensions of tax policy that are to be chosen under all relevant contingencies. The resulting political cost of giving up discretion over contemporary tax policy appears to be too high relative to the benefit of foreclosing time inconsistency.

---

[35] On retrospective voting see, for example, Ferejohn (1986) and Achen and Bartels (2016).

[36] Howitt's argument is made in the context of his discussion of pensions.

[37] The associated problem posed by the existence of powerful independent agencies is studied by Tucker (2018).

[38] Blinder (1997) also asks this question.

A more radical solution is a constitutional amendment to better protect property rights. An example of the difference that constitutional protection makes can be seen in the different institutional forms that arise across water and electric utilities in Canada versus the United States (Baldwin 2022). In Canada, the lack of constitutional protection for private property led to governmental encroachment on its contracts with private utility providers, leading eventually to their restructuring in the form of public utilities. In the United States, where the right to private property is enshrined in its constitution, regulated private utilities are the norm instead. It is interesting to observe that Canada had a chance to put private property into the constitution in 1982 when it was finally repatriated from the United Kingdom. The issue was debated, but no such amendment was introduced. Is this choice about property rights and the absence of central taxing a failure of policy making, or are they sensible courses of action given the consequences of the implied constraints on discretionary action in a democracy?

4.3 Problems Due to the Differences between Markets and Elections

In our discussion of the standard of reference appropriate for a liberal democracy, we observed that constraints required to limit the authority of the state will also reduce the operating efficiency of the public sector. In this section we deal with three issues that further complicate our assessment of the quality of electoral outcomes: international competition among governments, domestic special interest politics, and the common pool problem in public finance.

4.3.1 International Competition

As soon as we extend our analysis of electoral competition to an international setting, it becomes obvious that international competition creates problems for allocation through the political process. Consumers can purchase goods in foreign as well as in domestic markets, and private firms can operate in international markets as well as at home. But the same extension does not apply to the corresponding political elements because voting, the domain of political parties and of an electoral system are all defined strictly on a national basis. Consequently, parties will not take the implications of their domestic decisions for global social welfare fully into account. Widespread concern with some global issues and the working of international organizations may blunt the force of this observation. But it is an open question as to how well they will serve as a substitute for democratic world government.[39]

Harmonization is one response to the harmful consequences of international fiscal competition. The approach has a long history going back at least to Seligman in the 1920s (Musgrave 1988). The idea is to create conditions that allow distinct national policy choices to coexist without distorting international flows of goods and factors, while at the same time attenuating the incentives countries have to engage in discriminatory fiscal practices, thereby preventing "social dumping" of bad jobs and a "race to the bottom" in tax rates. This sort of policy harmonization requires adoption by international agreement of certain principles of taxation, such as the destination rather than the origin principle for commodity taxation, and the residence rather than source principle for income taxation. It also includes the single tax principle – that a taxpayer should be taxed only once, and at least once – leading to international cooperation to prevent tax evasion, such as the recent (2021) agreement to impose a global minimum corporate income tax.

Harmonization is complicated by the many avenues that states have for engaging in predatory practices. Sinn (2003, chapter 2) suggests that tax harmonization will just lead to more use of other, nontax policy instruments, such as infrastructure spending, as countries try to maintain an advantage over their trading partners. Others point to the complications that follow from the insistence by nation states on taxation of resource and other rents at their source. These problems heighten the challenges posed by unregulated international competition among sovereign governments, and further prejudice the case against such competition as a beneficial process.

An alternative, less discussed, approach to international competition emphasizes the dangers of using fiscal coordination to shelter countries from international competition. From this perspective harmonization shelters domestic rents, whereas international competition forces tax prices down toward the marginal cost of providing public services to mobile users. Mueller (2000, 182) observes that citizens move toward jurisdictions with high taxes that fund high-quality public services. He argues that the typical advocate of harmonization "knows what the proper level of taxation for a country should be and how this money should be spent", and fears that any loss in tax revenue due to international tax competition will harm these programs. He concludes, "Such fears are unfounded, if governments provide the goods and services that their citizens want and use benefit taxation." Vanberg (2000, 100) adds that in this

---

[39] On the consequences of international tax competition, see Wilson (1999), Haufler (2001), Fuest, Huber and Mintz (2005), and Keen and Konrad (2013). Wildasin (2021) surveys open economy public economics from a more general perspective.

context, using benefit taxation means that tax contributions should be regarded as a price willingly paid for benefits, which in the judgment of taxpayers offset the costs, "in the light of available alternative options."[40]

Vanberg does not rule out the possibility that some rules about how international competition is to be conducted may be desirable. Nonetheless, while international arbitrage is commonly regarded as a significant constraint on domestic policy choices, the two normative approaches embody quite different perspectives on the social utility of intergovernmental competition.

4.3.2 Special Interest Politics

We have pointed out that the scale of organization required to influence public policy is substantial when compared to that of altering personal product choice in a market. This characteristic of the polity makes it possible for small, organized groups to direct resources toward themselves despite the socially harmful consequences of the policies they seek. The classic case involves a relatively easily organized group of producers who profit from a policy-induced increase in product prices at the expense of many consumers who each suffer to an extent that is too small to provoke them into active opposition. An example of this kind, which even appears in Pareto's "Manual" (1971, 379), involves a tariff on an imported consumer good. The literature on the political economy of taxation is full of cases in which individual welfare losses for consumers aggregate to an amount that exceeds the benefit to producers (see, for example, Shugart 1997).

Regulations on entry into an industry that protect rents enjoyed by existing firms and industrial subsidies for them are further examples of policies with concentrated benefits and diffuse costs (Stigler 1971; Peltzman 1976). Migué (1977) explains the choice between entry controls and industry subsidies: the first order of business is always to reduce the elasticity of supply, followed by subsidies once entry barriers ensure that they will not be competed away by new entrants. In declining industries where entry is not a threat, subsidies are preferred at the outset, though they may not completely offset the source of their troubles (Hillman 1982). Olson (1982) goes further to argue that as a democracy matures and special interests proliferate, economic growth declines because interest groups resist sectoral reallocations that diminish their policy-generated rents.

The existence of inefficient policies in response to special interest lobbies in the framework of the model in Section 3 stems from (1) the use of political

---

[40] Since true benefit taxation is not feasible, we interpret this to refer to the fiscal system in a well-functioning competitive political economy.

resources $C(s)$ to influence policy actions, and (2) a way for these resources to enhance political support even though the government does not take the full economic consequences of the policies supplied into account, a situation depicted earlier in (4.1). These resources may be transferred to political parties or used in various ways by lobbyists to influence legislative decisions; may rise to equal the size of the rents created on behalf of special interests; and are considered by some to be an additional source of social welfare loss (Tullock 1967; Kreuger 1974). Dixit, Grossman, and Helpman (1997) conclude that if there are many interests that can be played off against each other, and the cost of doing so is low, much of the rent will be transferred to the government.

In a challenge to the conclusion that special interests distort public policy, Wittman (1995) admonishes readers not to confuse interests with influence. He points out that even small losses of support from citizens who are part of a large, diffuse majority can, when totaled, easily outweigh the gain in support from granting a preferential policy to a small interest group.

Does electoral competition squeeze out inefficient policies of the sort we are discussing? An affirmative answer is provided by Becker who, we recall, regards political competition as a veil for rivalry among interest groups. In Becker's view, the equilibrium outcome depends on who stands to gain the most. Competition among interest groups then leads to the survival of policies that raise output and welfare because favorably affected groups find it in their interest to lobby more for these policies than unfavorably affected groups will lobby against. The outcome replicates a social benefit–cost analysis in which the gains and losses for different groups are weighted according to their political influence.[41] Opposition by organized groups may not even be necessary for efficiency if individual voters are aware of the consequences of the policies that special interests seek, and care about their own welfare (Hinich and Munger 1994, 182). Both of these conditions hold in the model of the well-functioning polity presented in Section 3.

Businesses that try to influence public policy often hire professional lobbyists. de Figueiredo and Richter (2014, 163) inform us that in 2012, $3.5 billion was spent on lobbying politicians in the United States, more than five times the total amount spent on campaign contributions.[42] There is no doubt that lobbying serves the interests of the lobbyists' clients. What is more difficult to ascertain is

---

[41] Resources used in this process may be thought of as transaction costs that accompany allocation through the public sector. Rent seeking will add to these costs. Such reasoning may lead on to a transaction cost perspective on the question of whether to assign a particular function to the public or to the private sector that is in the tradition initiated by Coase (1960).

[42] See Ansolabehere, de Figueiredo, and Snyder (2003) on the (surprisingly little) money in elections.

whether it worsens the allocation of resources (Bombardini and Trebbi 2020). Lobbying may be an essential means of information transmission.[43] Achen and Bartels (2016, 321) suggest that if voters are to have their interests represented, interest groups and parties, which (we add) are more instrumental than individual voters, must do much of the work. Stigler (1971, 97) suggests that these agents will become more important, the more rapidly and unpredictably the interests of the electorate change. If information transmission is the essence of this activity, and/or if lobbying works as in Becker's framework, it may improve overall welfare. A critical issue is whether there is an asymmetry of knowledge between voters and lobbyists that can be manipulated for selfish reasons. This is one reason we have discussed the information question at length in Section 4.1.

4.3.3 The Common Pool Problem

A public good problem arises when the benefits from private contributions to its supply are nonexcludable and so received by all. Private suppliers in a market cannot then be adequately compensated and there is a need for public action. In contrast, a common pool problem arises when benefits derived from exploitation of a resource are private to the user, while the associated costs are public and so imposed on everyone. In this case, there is a need for *inaction*, that is, for greater restraint in resource exploitation (Ostrom 1990; Sandler and Arce 2003).

The common pool problem we are concerned with arises when politicians spend money from a general revenue fund fed by taxes levied on the country as a whole. A common tax pool allows "some people [to] spend other people's money" without fully accounting for the consequences of the taxation of private incomes (von Hagen 2006, 464). The immediate cause is the diffusion of authority within political parties and governments, which makes the coordination needed to match spending with taxation difficult. In the competitive political economy of Section 3, the governing party is a single responsible authority. Taxes paid by every taxpayer are politically salient, and the successful party presents a set of policies that reconciles both sides of the budget, at least as far as possible given the difficulties of levying individualized tax-prices. In reality, however, the government is a collection of semiautonomous agents or parties. Under proportional representation (PR), a governing coalition typically involves several parties, each with its own core supporters. In a majoritarian system where one party usually governs alone, there are many elected

---

[43] For models of lobbying as information transmission, see, for example, Austen-Smith and Wright (1996) and Skaperdas and Vaidya (2021). Basu (2000, chapter 7) discusses the policy advising process when information is costly and asymmetrically possessed.

representatives who form the caucus of the party and who each have some agency despite their party membership.

Persson, Roland, and Tabellini (2007) show how the common pool problem may be modeled using a spatial probabilistic voting framework. Here we illustrate it by adapting a diagram used by Inman and Rubinfeld (2020, 144). Figure 1 is drawn for various levels of public outlay G arising within one of many electoral districts, $n = 1, 2, ..., N$, in a majoritarian electoral system or, alternatively, for a group of core supporters of party n that is part of a governing coalition under PR. The marginal benefit of public outlay curve slopes downward to reflect diminishing marginal returns to consumption. The marginal social cost of G is assumed to be constant for convenience.

The actual marginal tax cost to taxpayers in district n, or to supporters of coalition member n, is a fraction λ of the full cost since that cost is spread through the tax system across taxpayers in the whole country. If all political agents achieve their politically optimal level G_n', which is greater than the

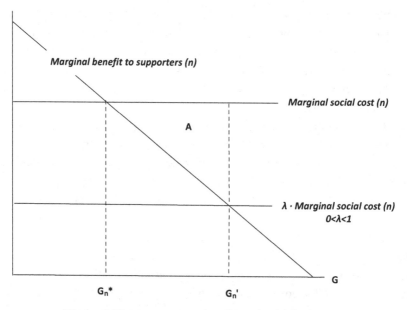

Figure 1 The common pool problem in public finance

Note: n denotes a particular electoral district in a majoritarian electoral system, or a particular party in a governing coalition under PR. *Marginal social cost (n)* is the full marginal social cost of supplying good G to the nth district, or to supporters of the nth member of a governing coalition. $\lambda \cdot$ *Marginal social cost (n)*, $0 < \lambda < 1$, is the marginal cost of benefits to voters in district n, or to supporters of the nth coalition member, when the full cost is spread over all taxpayers through the national tax system.

socially optimal level G_n* in each case, the resulting total social loss from overexploitation of the national tax base will be equal to N times area A.

With each member of the governing party, or each part of the governing coalition, treating everyone else's supporters like fish in international waters, the question arises as to how the resulting struggle is resolved. One answer by Weingast (1979), Shepsle and Weingast (1981), and others is that each risk-averse legislator or coalition partner prefers an outcome that gives to every member their politically optimal choice G_n'. They prefer this solution to the risky alternative under which each of them tries to shift more of the tax burden onto the supporters of their colleagues by engineering a smaller winning coalition; when decisions are subject to majority-rule approval, small winning coalitions are inherently unstable.

The solution in which everyone gets a piece of the action is referred to as the norm of universalism. When this outcome characterizes actual budgetary outcomes, we should expect higher levels of public spending in situations where there are larger numbers of key decision makers. There is, in fact, evidence that expenditure grows with the size of the legislature in US states (Gilligan and Matsusaka 1995), with the council size in US city governments (Baqir 2002), and with legislature size in the world (Bradbury and Crain 2001). Related work discussed by Inman and Rubinfeld (2020, chapter 5) considers how smaller sized US state senates can constrain spending by larger elected legislatures. There is also evidence that coalition governments spend more than single-party majority governments (Persson, Roland and Tabellini 2007). Consequently, the fact that PR leads to party fragmentation and thus more coalition government, as Duverger (1954) predicts, makes it unsurprising that PR governments are often observed to spend more than majoritarian ones do (Persson and Tabellini 2008).[44]

Since universalism leads to overuse of the tax pool and a loss of social welfare, we should also expect that interparty competition will give rise to arrangements that allow governing parties to profit from the support that can be realized by taming the problem. Strategies that have been used include delegation to, or control by, strong ministers of finance, usually found in electoral systems with single-party governments, and coordination or contract devices

---

[44] This observation should be distinguished from the consequences for the *structure* of public expenditure of different electoral systems. As Persson and Tabellini (2000, chapter 8), McKenzie (2001), and others argue, in majoritarian systems (under PR), competition leads parties to focus on geographically defined marginal constituencies (on broadly defined social groups). Thus, as shown empirically by Milesi-Ferretti, Perotti, and Rostagno (2002) and Scartascini and Crain (2021), majoritarian governments (PR governing coalitions) spend more on targetable goods and services (on transfers that can be targeted to social groups). There also appears to be more redistribution in PR systems (Iversen and Soskice 2006).

more appropriate for situations involving coalition government, since delegation within a coalition is difficult to organize and enforce.

Party leaders may try to get their colleagues to internalize the spending
externality using high-powered incentive schemes, such as offering their presence and financial support in re-election campaigns in return for moderating
spending demands, or appointment to a higher position within the party structure. These measures aim to increase λ in the thinking of individual decision
makers. In terms of Figure 1, this involves shifting the lower horizontal line
upward. It should be easier to do this if the party enjoys political support from
all segments of the electorate, because this heightens the political saliency of all
the welfare losses depicted in Figure 1.[45]

Less ambitiously, the tendency toward overexpansion may be kept in check
by simply bounding the loss. This alternative strategy is represented in Figure 1
by a leftward shift of the vertical line through the point G_n'. For example, in a
majoritarian Westminster system, control over the budget is given to the minister of finance who, making use of the doctrines of cabinet solidarity and budget
secrecy, says "No" to the ministers of spending departments (Breton 1996,
chapter 4). Cabinet solidarity prevents disappointed ministers from going to
supporters outside of the cabinet after a budget is decided upon, while budget
secrecy gives the upper hand to the minister of finance in his or her negotiations
with spending departments that do not know the whole plan.[46] According to
Breton, these conventions along with a line-item veto allows a government in a
Westminster system to match spending with taxing more effectively that the
president in the US congressional system can. de Figueiredo (2003) extends this
argument to show how strengthening of the executive's use of the line-item veto
responds to expected changes in the scale of the common pool problem.

Since coalition government often arises in PR systems, the contract approach
is more likely to emerge there. This may include budgetary agreements among
coalition members on ex ante fiscal targets. Such arrangements may require
monitoring by the minister of finance, in which case the distinction between
delegation and contracting is less meaningful.

Empirical evidence suggests that, to an extent that varies across the cases
considered, arrangements involving delegation and contracting both do have
some of their intended effect, as shown by Hallerberg, Strauch, and von Hagen
(2009), de Haan, Jong-A-Pin, and Mierau (2013), and others. This judgment
also applies to balanced budget laws and other ex ante fiscal rules that have been

---

[45] As far as we can determine this hypothesis has not yet been explored.

[46] Dixit (1996) cautions that there may be trade-offs between low-powered and high-powered
    incentives. In our context, saying "No" too often may compromise the prime minister when
    appealing to spending ministers to internalize the fortunes of the party.

adopted in both majoritarian and PR systems (e.g., von Hagen 2006; Hou and Smith 2010; Atkinson and Mou 2016).

Decentralization, Yardstick Competition, and Foot Voting

Federalism – decentralization to governments within geographical areas of the responsibility for supplying *and* financing selected public services – is another way of dealing with the common pool problem by confining it to a smaller area within which there is, in principle, a closer though still imperfect matching of costs and benefits. Even highly centralized countries have some degree of federalism with respect to urban government.[47]

Federalism also substantially enhances two competitive forces that play a role in sanctioning local or subcentral governments. They are of particular interest in the context of this study. The first of these is yardstick competition: the interregional competition forced upon local governments because of the enhanced ability that decentralization creates for citizens to observe what is going on in other places, which then forms a basis for retrospective voting on government performance (Salmon 1987, 2019; Besley and Case 1995). The second follows from the constitutionally protected ability of citizens to migrate freely across jurisdictional boundaries within the same country in response to differences in net fiscal benefits. In contrast to yardstick competition, migration, or "foot voting" (Tiebout 1956; Somin 2020), involves individuals acting to improve their own welfare without the intermediation of politics.

The importance of yardstick competition and foot voting as disciplining devices depends on the cost of migration. Yardsticks are likely to decline in relative importance as migration becomes less costly. If the cost of moving is low enough, even the threat of foot voting will remove the incentive to pursue a unique local policy and mobile factors will be treated equally everywhere, though this may be equally badly. When migration costs are treated more realistically, analyses of the quality of a migration equilibrium in a federal system struggle to find a place between the same polar views described in our remarks on international competition: that it leads to a race to the bottom, or that it results in an efficient allocation of policy instruments and economic resources among jurisdictions. See, for example, Breton and Scott (1978, chapter 10), Wellisch (2000, chapter 6), Treisman (2007, chapter 4), and Harrison (2006).

The use of yardstick comparisons is problematic if mobility generates a geographical sorting of voters, as Bishop (2008) claims is true for the United

---

[47] For this decentralization to work, the central government must be able to resist strategic attempts by subcentral ones to get it to pay for local programs – the soft budget constraint problem. Literature on this problem is reviewed by Treisman (2007, chapter 5) and Revelli and Bracco (2020, chapter 7).

States. In the same situation, the value of foot voting as a disciplining device is also reduced (Caplan 2001). Moreover, when thinking about these processes as disciplining devices we should remember that political parties are not residual claimants to the net gains that follow from their policy choices and will propose internalization of decision externalities only when their fortunes can be improved through the political process, a qualification that, in general, also applies to all of the disciplining devices that we have discussed. In summarizing his survey of the empirical evidence on yardstick competition, Salmon (2019, 123) writes that while "[s]ome of the findings ... are negative, ... the general message seems clear: empirical evidence does support the view that yardstick competition and yardstick voting are operative, and play a role, at least sometimes."

One should also note that while yardstick competition and foot voting may sanction local governments to some extent, their relationship to the common pool problem is not clear. On the one hand, they permit citizens to uncover, and to protect themselves from, situations in which they are asked to pay for services they do not receive. On the other hand, these processes may lead to more pressure for local governments to shift the cost of the services they provide to other places. The matter again resolves into questions about the quality of a federal fiscal equilibrium.

Designing federations with a view to producing outcomes that are as good as possible is a challenge for institutional engineers. Inman and Rubinfeld (2020) discuss the design issues from different perspectives. Reform of a federation is infrequent of course because its structure is usually specified in a constitution that is not easily amended. (Urban or regional government is another matter.) Nonetheless, there is probably much that can be learned by comparing existing federations such as Australia, Canada, the United States, the European Union, and South Africa with respect to the effectiveness of yardstick and foot voting and their ability to constrain the common pool problem.

5 Fiscal Structure

"If participants make no linkage between the tax and benefit sides of the account, taxes would simply never be observed" (Buchanan 1976, 21). However, the difficulty of levying taxes on individuals in accordance with benefits received, and the necessity of divorcing benefits from taxes paid in order to redistribute, leads to thinking about taxation as a matter that is distinct from the financing of public services. In this section, we proceed in this way. We add to our characterization of the structure of the public sector by considering how *tax structures* emerge in a competitive electoral equilibrium. We then explore the implications of this logic for its consistency with some ideas about complexity that have emerged from various parts of the normative tax literature.

5.1 Tax Structure as a Sorting Equilibrium[48]

All tax systems exhibit the same basic structure: economic activities are grouped into tax bases; various nominal rates are levied on these bases; and special provisions such as deductions, exemptions, and credits are created that alter the definition of the bases and produce divergences between nominal and effective tax rates. Special provisions are often called loopholes (especially when the writer thinks they ought not to exist.) In a political economy analysis, this structure emerges as a political equilibrium that evolves through time. An analysis of this sort thus differs from more traditional approaches that are based on a normative criterion of what tax systems should be like for equity, efficiency, and related reasons. A tax structure emerges endogenously, rather than being imposed exogenously on the basis of expert opinion from outside. Such opinion may enter as an influence on voters or politicians, but it will represent merely one element that they consider.

In the model introduced in Section 3, political parties that maximize expected support will aim for a tax structure that equalizes the marginal political cost or expected loss in votes from raising another dollar of revenue across tax instruments. In the absence of administration and other transaction costs, the resulting tax system would look like the one described in (3.6), with a separate tax rate for each voter. If we were to allow explicitly for each voter to engage in different kinds of taxable activities, the complexity of the tax system would increase accordingly.

Once it is acknowledged that fiscal systems are costly to administer, political cost minimization makes it possible to understand how a tax structure consisting of bases, rate structures, and special provisions arises (Yitzhaki 1979; Hettich and Winer 1988; Warskett, Winer, and Hettich 1998). To economize on the cost of operating a tax system and to provide more of the goods and services demanded, governments will group related activities into composite bases. This lowers the costs of becoming informed about the particulars of individual taxpayers, of designing elaborate tax structures, and enforcing tax laws. In an analogous manner, taxpayers will be grouped into rate bands rather than each having a unique rate. However, grouping taxpayers by economic and political margins creates a loss in expected political support since the differentiated treatment of heterogeneous taxpayers would maximize support in a frictionless world. Successful parties will balance this loss against the gain in support by

---

[48] This section relies on Winer (2019).

spending fewer resources on administrative activities and more on the provision of public services.

A similar argument can be used to explain the existence of special provisions. If there is a group that offers effective political opposition to the inclusion of a specific activity in a particular base, it may be cheaper to placate it with a special provision, rather than by creating a separate base for the disputed item. For example, capital gains may be made part of a broadly defined income tax but taxed at a rate that differs from the rate applied to other types of income. Note that in this framework special provisions are a rational response by governing parties that are competing with opposition parties. They are not deviations from some ideal tax base designed to satisfy normative criteria, nor are they only introduced as hidden or otherwise undesirable substitutes for direct subsidies, as is sometimes argued in tax expenditure literature.[49] Special tax provisions would exist even in a world where no attempt is made to subsidize favored activities. Moreover, special provisions may be adjusted, and with more precision than tax rates, to reflect variation in assessments of the worth of public services among distinct groups of taxpayers, making "loopholes" important avenues through which spending and taxing for individuals is brought closer together.

The tax structure that emerges from these considerations is a sorting equilibrium formed in the face of information and administration costs. It follows that changes in preferences for public goods and services and in the relative political influence of various groups will alter that equilibrium. Because revenue structures are equilibrium outcomes, they will adjust whenever unanticipated shocks occur. If the size of a potential base expands, for example, the marginal excess burden of relying more heavily on that tax source will fall relative to using other bases. Relying more heavily on the now larger base also disperses political opposition across a wider economic space (Kenny and Winer 2006).

Structural adjustment to an expanding (or declining) base – a normal tax change – is neither a sign of political instability nor evidence of tax reform as that term is conventionally understood. Thus the worldwide movement to extend consumption taxation to services as that sector in Western economies grows in relative size is understandable and would likely have occurred even in the absence of normative arguments about the inefficiency of manufacturers' sales taxes.[50] The value-added tax (VAT) form of consumption taxation that has been widely adopted also maintains the taxation of imports in place of tariff

---

[49] On the definition of a tax expenditure as a revenue loss relative to a Schanz–Haig-Simons broad base income tax, see Surrey (1973).

[50] Why the degree of VAT coverage across commodities varies internationally remains to be explained.

revenues which declined with freer international trade after the Second World War.

In addition to the base effect, there is also one that depends on the scale of the public sector. As the demand for public services grows, all revenue sources will be relied upon to a greater extent, with the mix of taxes depending on the relative political cost associated with each revenue source. Judgments about these political costs will, as always, be influenced by both the economic consequences of alternative policy choices as well as the relative political influence of the groups on which they fall.

By identifying a scale effect, we do not mean to imply that causality goes only from government size to tax structure. Expenditures and taxes are interdependent. One can ask if an exogenous shock that leads to greater efficiency in taxation (e.g., the *invention* of VAT) also leads to bigger government; or if causality runs from factors underlying the demand for government to tax structure. There is some empirical evidence that the adoption of VAT led to modest government growth (Keen and Lockwood 2006) and, more generally, that reduction of the deadweight costs of taxation has led to growth of the public sector (Becker and Mulligan 2003). On the other hand, Lee, Kim, and Borcherding (2013) find that the causal effect of tax structure on government size is small compared to the effect of exogenous changes in factors determining the demands for public services.[51]

We can also go further with respect our understanding of changes in tax systems that are often associated with, or identified as, "tax reform" (Hettich and Winer 2006). In a tax system that is continually evolving in response to shocks, technical "reforms" will occur as new situations are encountered and adjusted to and coordinating "reform" will occur from time to time to co-ordinate actions across tax and other government departments after many piecemeal technical changes have been made. Comprehensive "reform" of the sort proposed by special commissions is observed even more infrequently, driven by important structural changes in the economy and in the distribution of political influence. In the longer run, the evolution of tax systems will also be shaped by the character of basic political institutions (Steinmo 1993, 2003; Kenny and Winer 2006; Besley and Persson 2011).

We should then ask, are observed tax systems efficient (as the preceding discussion in this section could be read as implying)? In a well-functioning, perfectly competitive polity they would be, and we can see, here and there, examples of the logic of the well-functioning polity reflected in the shape of

---

[51] Hoover and Sheffrin (1992) discuss the issues involved in determining causality while investigating the relationship between taxing and spending in the United States.

actual tax systems. For example, income tax systems with means-tested benefits tend to have U-shaped marginal tax rate structures that are compatible with optimal tax considerations – high marginal rates on lower-income people as transfers are phased out, lower marginal rates for middle-income earners to avoid work disincentives, and rising rates as one moves further up the income scale to enhance progressivity (Abdel-Khadar and De Mooij 2021, 2c). We also see the movement toward tax mixes that keep the burden of taxation low as the economy evolves and as public expenditure expands, which may be why we do not see substantial adverse economic consequences associated closely with public sector size. For example, the large public sectors of the Nordic countries are financed with heavy reliance on consumption taxes and with dual income tax systems that tax mobile capital lightly in these small open economies.[52]

On the other hand, the political process is an imperfect allocation mechanism for the reasons we have discussed. A challenging task facing students of political economy is to link these problems to specific aspects of actual fiscal systems and other public policies. We have done so only in a limited fashion, as with the discussions of time inconsistency and special interest politics.

5.2 Dealing with Complexity

Simplifying a tax system is a complicated matter because it involves many trade-offs among economic and political objectives (James, Sawyer, and Budak 2016). Moreover, taxpayers are reluctant to ignore the special circumstances that they find themselves in, as evidence in Blesse, Buhlmann, and Doerrenberg (2021) indicates. Nor, as we see it, do politicians want to substantially change the means they have devised to generate and maintain support in a competitive system.

In contrast to this perspective, there is a predisposition to reduce or avoid complexity in most normative theories and applications. The Meade Report (IFS 1977, 44) expressed the view of many public finance scholars when it argued against a fully optimal tax system that makes many economically relevant distinctions among economic activities even if it could be designed and implemented. This is because such a system would provide avenues for special interests to cater to their own interests rather than to the general welfare, "each obtaining some specific exemption or other advantage until the whole structure becomes a shambles of special provisions." It advocated adoption of a broad base expenditure tax among other reforms. Earlier, the Canadian Royal

---

[52] Lindert (2004) examines the connection between welfare state size and economic growth, while Beramendi and Rueda (2007) – see also references in their footnote 3 – study the relationship between consumption taxation and redistribution.

Commission on Taxation (1966) argued for a broad base income tax. Such broad bases are not fully optimal, but they are, more or less, neutral with respect to alternative economic activities. Social planning in its optimal tax application is often used to look for conditions under which somewhat simplified structures are efficient, even if they are more complex than a broad base expenditure or income tax.

The exchange-contractarian position also favors a simplified tax system, though for different reasons. Brennan and Buchanan (1980, 80–82) demonstrate that a fully optimal consumption tax designed under a revenue constraint is precisely one that maximizes the size of tax revenues by, for example, taxing inelastically demand goods relatively heavily, thereby maximizing the loss of welfare from an overexpanded public sector. Buchanan and Congleton (1998) argue for greater generality in taxation partly for this reason. Much earlier, Simons (1938) proposed a broad base income tax as a way of preserving individual liberty, by keeping the government from "dipping into great incomes with a sieve."[53] Simons (1936) was also an early advocate of a monetary rule.

The problem with simplified fiscal structures, and with delegation to independent agencies, is that they are not generally consistent with vigorous political competition. The degree of complexity of public policy, which might be measured by the number of distinctions made among activities that are relevant to the lives of citizens, may rise and fall over time, and is limited by information and coordination costs as well as by views about equity. But policy structures remain complex because the demands of the electorate are.

6 Political Competitiveness

We move from an analysis of the elements and effects of political competition to consider the measurement and consequences of changes in its degree. Our discussion emphasizes the multidimensionality of political competitiveness, illustrates the issues involved in deriving appropriate measures, and demonstrates that competitiveness in mature democracies has varied, often substantially. We then consider the consequences of changes in the degree of competition found in a variety of studies, of the US South, the OECD, Italian regions, and Indian states.

The question that arises at the outset is why the intensity of competition would vary in a mature democracy. There are at least three reasons: (1) Parties impose constraints on themselves to preserve their credibility and coherence and to cater to donors (Demsetz 1982; Levy 2004; Roemer

---

[53] Simons' concern for liberty also led him to advocate for progressive taxation as a means of ensuring the equality required for freedom of association (Hettich 1979).

2001). When circumstances change, some parties can adapt their programs faster than others; (2) In electoral systems with individual electoral districts, parties impose constraints on their local candidates to protect their national reputation, a situation studied by Austen-Smith (1987), Callander (2005), Winer, Kenny, and Grofman (2014), and others. This tether prevents local candidates from situating their own platforms close to their major opponent if this involves a substantial departure from the national party platform. Thus, a candidate's ability to be fully competitive locally will depend on tether length relative to the median and ideological dispersion of the local electorate. Since the length of tethers and the distribution of local electorates vary over time and space, so too will the number of contests in which candidates of both parties can fashion fully competitive platforms;[54] and (3) The institutional setting of elections may change in ways that enhance, or restrain, interparty rivalry. Voter registration laws may expand or contract the electorate, the boundary of electoral districts may be manipulated or depoliticized, campaign finance laws may be changed to limit or encourage private donations, and nonparty political advertising may be limited or encouraged.

The relative importance of these factors is not easy to establish. It seems likely that the institutional setting becomes more important as we go further into the history of what are now the mature, democratic countries and as our definition of democracy broadens.[55]

6.1 Measures of Competitiveness

The measurement of competitiveness is usually aimed at capturing the key factors that reflect the intensity of competition in elections, including the unpredictability of election outcomes and the degree of contestability that the field of opposing parties exhibits. Other measures focus on the responsiveness of government to changes in citizens' demand, and some deal with competitiveness in the legislature between elections. Each of these measures is a description of a distinct but related aspect of the same phenomenon. Our aim in the following discussion is to expose the ideas behind the measures that we present without using extensive mathematical descriptions. Detailed specifications are provided in the references cited.

---

[54] There may also be a size effect (Gerring et al. 2015). Electoral districts with more voters tend to be more heterogeneous, thus offering more cleavages for parties to exploit.

[55] For an introduction to the study of political competitiveness when nondemocratic regimes of various types are also included, see Hyde and Marinov (2012).

6.1.1 Competitiveness as Unpredictability or Closeness

The idea that a highly competitive election is one that is "too close to call" has a long tradition in the scholarly literature and in popular discourse, for a good reason: there is no meaningful contest if the outcome is always known with certainty. When deciding upon a measure of the closeness or unpredictability of an election, it is important to recognize that the underlying logic is ex ante: the expectation of outcomes must be formed prior to the outcome of the contest. If in operationalizing "too close to call" we simply replace the ex ante concept with its ex post result (plus a random term), we are implicitly invoking a strong form of rational expectations. No matter what information set is used in making predictions, all attempts at measurement must deal with this ex ante–ex post distinction.

The oldest and most well used measure of competitiveness as unpredictability is the observed first versus second place vote share margin, $v_1 - v_2$. In this case an election is seen as highly competitive if this vote share margin is "small" (e.g., Mayhew 1974; Jacobsen 2004). In Table 1 a related statistic, the (absolute value of the) deviation of the Republican share of the two-party vote in US Senate elections from one-half, averaged over twelve-year periods, is used to illustrate the distributional characteristics of the vote margins of the dominant two parties for open Senate elections (that did not involve an incumbent).[56] The table suggests that open Senate elections became considerably more competitive following the Second World War, especially in the 1960s. The post-2006 period exhibits a strong reversal of this trend, with outcomes concentrated in the upper tail of the distribution, where winning margins are relatively large for both Republican and Democratic candidates. An important take-away from the table is that competitiveness fluctuates substantially across time and, as we would see if the table were to be suitably disaggregated, across space, even though the United States is a mature democracy.

It is tempting to attribute the rise of competitiveness in the 1960s illustrated in the table to changes in voter registration and the decline after 2004 to party polarization. But caution should be exercised in drawing conclusions at least because a simple vote margin, however calculated, is not a good measure of closeness for at least three reasons. First, the significance of any vote share margin will be a function of how much variability, or volatility, there is in the proportion of the electorate that is likely to switch its vote from one election to the next (Przeworski and Sprague 1971; Elkins 1974). Even a relatively small margin can be associated with an election that is not close if the expected

---

[56] On vote margins in the US House, see Jacobsen (2006).

Table 1 Distribution of vote margins in Open[a] US Senate Elections: 1922–2016 |Republican share of the two-party vote − 0.5|[b]

Averages over 12-year periods	0.00–0.05	0.05–0.10	0.10 +
1922–33 48 states, 40 observations	25.0%	25.0%	50.0%
1934–45 48 states, 43 observations	27.9%	37.2%	34.9%
1946–57 48 states, 36 observations	36.1%	25.0%	38.9%
1958–69 50 states, 37 observations	64.9%	18.9%	16.2%
1970–81 49 states, 28 observations	41.1%	40.5%	18.4%
1982–93 49 states, 28 observations	46.4%	28.6%	25.0%
1994–2004 49 states, 30 observations	40.0%	43.3%	16.7%
2006–16 50 states, 41 observations	22.5%	24.0%	53.5%

Source: Winer, Kenny, and Grofman (2014, 474), extended through 2016 by the authors. B. Sanders is included in 2006. [a] Open = election with no incumbent.
[b] $|\{v_R/(v_R + v_D)\} - 0.5)|$.

volatility is, say, an order of magnitude smaller still. Volatility is usually measured by aggregating changes in the share of the vote experienced by each competing party over adjacent elections, taking care to avoid double counting. (On measuring volatility, see Bartolini and Mair 2007). Volatility may be incorporated by dividing each vote share margin by its associated vote volatility to derive a volatility-adjusted index.

A second problem, also emphasized by Przeworski and Sprague, is that even a volatility-adjusted first versus second place vote margin can be misleading if the winner faces competition from more than just the second-place finisher. The third problem stems from the difference between electoral turnover, which may not be affected even though margins fluctuate, and closeness. This last observation leads to measurement of the probability of loss of office and to consideration of the contestability of elections.

To deal with the second issue – accommodating all of the parties involved in a contest – we may define the margin or "distance to go" of each party (k) as the winner's vote share less the share of that party, $v_1 - v_k$, and then deflate that margin by the volatility in the district as a whole. A highly competitive district-level election in this context is one in which, for every party k, the "distance to go" is less than volatility. The resulting party-specific, volatility-adjusted margins may then be aggregated across parties for a given electoral district using party vote shares as weights, and then similarly aggregated up to the level of the legislature. Further detail about the construction of this index is provided in Dash, Ferris, and Winer (2019).

In Figure 2, which is based on election outcomes in fourteen major Indian states between 1967 and 2009, we compare the first versus second-place vote margin, this margin after it has been deflated by volatility, and the multiparty volatility-adjusted margin just defined. (As the world's largest democracy, India is an interesting case.) It is apparent from the figure that these indexes for Indian states do not reveal similar patterns. The unadjusted vote margin suggests that competitiveness within Indian state constituencies exhibited trend growth over time, whereas both the volatility-adjusted margin and the Przeworski/Sprague multiparty volatility-adjusted measure of competitiveness exhibit greater, but not the same, variability, and no trend. The same indexes constructed for Canadian national elections from 1867, shown in Ferris, Winer, and Grofman (2016), also exhibit differences in their patterns over the history of the modern Canadian state. In measuring competitiveness as uncertainty, incorporating volatility and allowing for more than two parties appears to be warranted.

The discussion so far focuses on majoritarian electoral systems. Blais and Lago (2009), and Grofman and Selb (2009) extend the measurement of vote share margins to proportional representation (PR). The PR system usually involves many candidates competing under a formula that apportions seats across parties depending on relative vote shares. As a competitiveness measure that they think may be applied to all electoral systems, Blais and Lago compute the minimal number of additional votes required under existing rules for *any* party to win an additional seat, divided by the number of ballots per seat to allow for the fact that it becomes more difficult to change the outcome of an election as the number of seats increases.[57] Competitiveness increases as this number falls. This measure resolves into the first versus second, party-level vote share margin in a majoritarian, single member plurality rule (SMP) system.[58] Grofman and Selb compute a similar number, but for each party, and then aggregate across parties using vote shares. Their measure too resolves into a vote share margin in an SMP system. These measures also vary across PR systems and, in Grofman and Selb's study, is also shown to vary over time.

---

[57] The calculation for a particular PR system depends on the exact seat distribution formula used.
[58] This result is problematic if measuring competitiveness in SMP systems requires an adjustment for volatility.

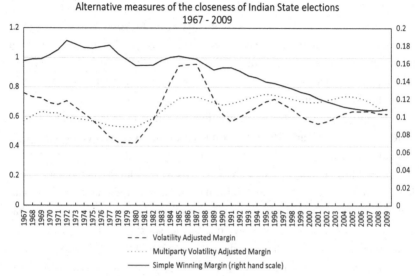

Alternative measures of the closeness of Indian State elections
1967 - 2009

– – – Volatility Adjusted Margin

· · · · · · Multiparty Volatility Adjusted Margin

——— Simple Winning Margin (right hand scale)

Figure 2 Alternative measures of the closeness of Indian state elections
1967–2009

Source: Dash, Ferris, and Winer (2019). The fourteen major states constitute about 85 percent of the Indian population. The first versus second volatility-adjusted margin = $(v_1 - v_2)/volatility$. The multiparty volatility-adjusted index is normalized to equal 1 at the constituency level if all party-specific vote share margins included are smaller than the corresponding vote volatility. Indexes are interpolated linearly between elections.

6.1.2 Competitiveness and the Asymmetry of Safe Seats

An alternative approach to measuring closeness focuses on the riskiness of the contest for political parties in the polity as a whole, rather than on unpredictability at the district level. It is well known that parties that compete across multiple districts in a majoritarian system will target marginal constituencies.[59] The strategy of targeting districts where the previous outcome can be most easily overturned suggests that the proportion of marginal seats (*MS*) is a useful measure of the degree of competitiveness. This measure can be improved by accounting for the fact that the party with relatively fewer marginal seats as a proportion of its total seat count, and hence with more safe seats, has an advantage in knowing where to target its resources. To do so, an adjustment in *MS* can be made that accounts for any asymmetry in the distribution of safe electoral districts among parties.

To classify seats as safe, we can follow Bodet (2014) and define a safe seat as one that lies in the upper tail of the distribution of the volatility-adjusted vote

---

[59] For a formal model that reaches this conclusion, see Persson and Tabellini (2000, chapter 8).

margins of incumbents. The proportion of marginal seats then is equal to $MS = 1 - \psi$, where ψ is the proportion of safe seats in a given election. Next we compute the Euclidean deviation from, say, a three-party equal sharing of safe seats as a measure of asymmetry (where the third party is "all other" than the two leaders), and normalize this to equal 1 if one party has all the safe seats, yielding ϕ_3. Finally an asymmetry-adjusted marginal seats measure for the election can be defined as $AMS = 1 - \{\psi\phi_3\}$. (See Dash, Ferris, and Winer 2019 for more detail.) This index can be computed for any majoritarian polity over time.

To illustrate the pattern of competitiveness that can be revealed by such a measure, we show in Figure 3 the change in AMS averaged across the fourteen Indian states used in Figure 2, while contrasting this index to changes in the unadjusted marginal seat index MS. The diagram indicates a considerable amount of variation in the marginal seat dimension of competitiveness, particularly in the later 1980s and early 1990s. Moreover, in the case of these Indian states, accounting for asymmetry in the distribution of safe seats among major parties reveals a smaller degree of variation in competitiveness than a focus purely on marginal seats would have recognized.

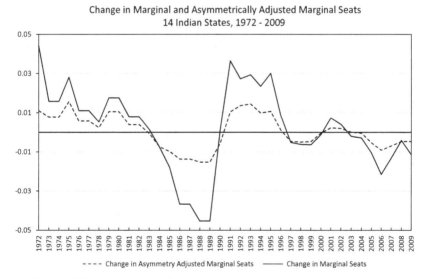

Figure 3 Change in marginal and asymmetry-adjusted marginal seats in fourteen Indian states, 1972–2009

Source: Dash, Ferris, and Winer (2019). A safe or non-marginal seat is one for which an incumbent's volatility-adjusted margin of victory over the nearest rival is one standard deviation above the mean of a rolling three past-election sample of such margins. Indexes are interpolated linearly between elections.

The same indexes over the history of Canada from 1867 are found in Ferris, Winer, and Grofman (2016). What marginal seat indexes look like for the US states referred to in Table 1 has not yet been investigated.

6.1.3 Competitiveness as the Incumbent's Probability of Loss

We conclude our overview of measures of competitiveness as unpredictability by considering closeness from the perspective of the incumbent party. Kayser and Lindstadt (2015) have constructed an index of the incumbent's electoral risk, whatever the electoral system, by estimating the probability that the governing party will lose the next election. Kayser and Lindstadt's measure depends upon: (1) estimation of the elasticity of seats with respect to votes (the swing ratio) under SMP, assumed to equal 1 under PR; and (2) estimation of the distribution of vote swings based on the entire history of such swings. These two are combined to estimate the probability of a seat swing large enough to close the seat gap between the incumbent and its main challenger, thus opening the door to a turnover of power. They avoid problems associated with third parties that might win, or with coalition formation, by assuming (in accordance with the record) that only two major parties or coalitions will ever form a government.

In Figure 4, we present from Splinter (2019) the Kayser and Lindstadt probability of loss measures of competitiveness for Canada from 1896 to 2011 together with Springer's recalculation of this measure using historical rather than estimated swing ratios and rolling estimates of seat swings based on several previous elections. While the calculated probabilities do differ in their levels, the methods agree in the pattern across time. Kayser and Lindstadt's (2015, 247) table illustrates the variation in loss probabilities that exists across a large sample of democracies with different electoral systems.

Cronert and Nyman (2021, 339) extend Kayser and Lindstadt's loss probability measure to allow for the possibility that in PR systems especially, but also in others, success in an election need not lead to participation in government. Their generalization requires estimation of the probability that a party enters government (or loses office) through the formation of different coalitions, which can be a complicated calculation.[60]

---

[60] In their most general formulation, the probability that a party p gains office is the sum of the probabilities of gaining office in any election outcome E_v weighted by the probability that election outcome will arise: $\text{Prob}(\text{Office})_p = \Sigma_{v=1}^{v=n} \text{Prob}(\text{Office}_v | E_v) \cdot \text{Prob}(E_v)$.

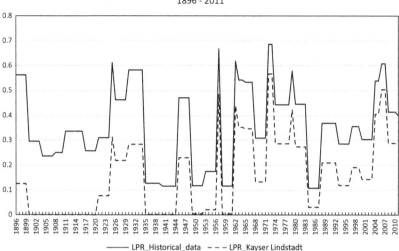

Figure 4 Loss Probabilities for Canada: 1896–2011

Source: Splinter (2019). Thesis data spreadsheet: columns AL and AM. Historical data refers to the use of actual rather than estimated swing ratios and, in this case, estimated seat swings are based on rolling estimates that use eight to eleven previous elections.

6.1.4 Contestability

Contestability refers to the existence of, or potential for, credible challengers to the governing party. This dimension of competitiveness is not simply another aspect of closeness since the opposition may be credible even though the government is in no danger of defeat in the next election. It is not clear how this dimension should be measured.

Sometimes reasoning about competition in private markets is carried over to the electoral context with the conclusion that contestability in a given jurisdiction rises with the number of parties. Such reasoning in the political context is, we think, wrong. In private goods markets, the entry of new firms signals the loss of market power for existing firms and allows firm rivalry to benefit consumers by either increasing their dimensions of choice, lowering market price, or both. On the other hand, the winner-takes-all nature of a majoritarian election (we consider proportional elections later) means that the entry of additional parties will decrease the likelihood that any one challenger will be a credible rival to the incumbent because entry usually fragments the vote. Moreover, the larger set of policy choices that comes from the enlarged set of parties is less meaningful than in a market because in the end, only one platform or menu of policies can be implemented. The situation is different in a market where there is room for many "restaurants" serving food.

This reasoning implies that in majoritarian electoral systems, fewer rather than more parties lead to more contestability by increasing the likelihood of there being a credible challenger. Contestability may be high even when there are only two parties, or even if there is just a credible potential challenger, as Demsetz (1968) argues is the case in a market even under conditions of natural monopoly, though the high fixed cost of party entry suggests that high contestability in an electoral system requires an actual rather than a potential rival. In this Duverger–Demsetz view of contestability, as Ferris, Winer, and Grofman (2016) refer to it, the pressure on voters to desert small parties with little chance of winning, which tends to reduce the number of parties, is a factor that helps to maintain contestability over time.

Thus, for majoritarian systems, the market-based conclusion that more parties necessarily mean more competition is inverted. One can argue that the situation in proportional electoral systems varies only in degree. Proportional representation allows parties to form around more distinctive ideological positions by allowing a larger number of parties to survive. Because only the winning coalition decides on the policies to be implemented, however, unlike a market where each firm can supply a different menu of products, voters are still concerned with the fact that minor party proposals are less likely to be implemented. Hence despite the greater persistence of minority interests in the legislature under PR, the same type of Duvergerian pressure winnows the political positions that can survive in equilibrium.

In Figure 5, we illustrate how contestability, measured imperfectly here as the effective number of political parties (*ENP*), has varied over the 1962–2017 period for five different countries, chosen to represent a variety of different electoral systems.[61] *ENP* weights parties by their relative size to capture both their number and their size distribution (Laakso and Taagepera 1979): $ENP = 1/\Sigma\ v_i^2$ where v_i is the vote share or seat share of party i. Economists will recognize this index as the inverse of the Hirschman–Herfindahl index (HHI) of market power with vote or seat shares of parties used in place of market shares of firms. The Duverger–Demsetz view suggests that contestability is at a maximum in SMP systems when two parties share the vote equally, in which case *ENP = 2*.

Both the United States and Canada have single-member plurality elections, with Canada having a parliamentary system and the United States a presidential one. Duverger's Law – that under SMP the party structure will converge on 2 – is most strongly apparent for the United States while Canada exhibits more

---

[61] Alternatives to ENP are considered in Ferris, Winer, and Grofman (2016). All of them are incomplete as a measure of contestability.

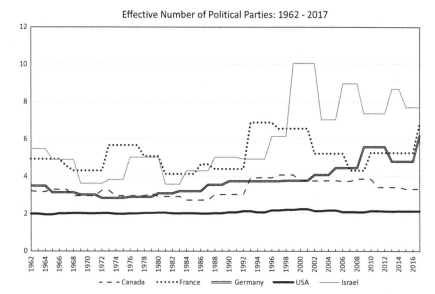

Figure 5 Effective number of political parties: 1962–2017
Source: Gallagher and Mitchell (2009) Election indices dataset online: www.tcd.ie/
Political_Science/people/michael_gallagher/ElSystems/index.php, Accessed 11/1/2021.

persistent departures from 2. Israel, with its PR system, has a much larger number of parties. France and Germany are intermediate cases: France has a mixed presidential and parliamentary system based on a two-round voting procedure, while Germany uses a mixed member proportional voting system (MMP), where both geographic and polity-wide party interests are reflected in proportional seating.

In addition to illustrating the variation in *ENP* that arises across electoral systems and over time, Figure 5 illustrates the well-known characteristic that electoral systems using PR or MMP typically have a larger number of parties surviving over time in comparison to majoritarian, plurality-rule systems. This observation is consistent with the view that PR systems produce greater party heterogeneity at the cost of contestability, while parliamentary and presidential systems lead to more contestable elections and, hence, greater accountability of elected governments.

However, Gehl and Porter (2020) suggest caution in interpreting small party numbers as evidence of greater competitiveness and accountability. They note that while smaller numbers may heighten contestability, the same Duvergerian logic that delivers small numbers also allows for greater collusion among parties to restrict the entry of challengers. The need to incorporate this trade-off into a more complete measure of contestability remains an outstanding challenge. A partial solution is provided by the indexes suggested by Gerring and colleagues (2018) and Skilling and Zeckhauser (2002). The former combine closeness and turnover in an index based on the difference in vote or seat shares between the incumbent and its largest challenger, while the latter use the inverse of ENP, that is, the HHI index, with the length of time a party or coalition is in office as its basic element. The potential for collusion is, however, only indirectly captured in these alternatives.

Buchler's (2011, chapter 6) argument that relatively homogeneous electoral districts in which one party dominates are better because they minimize the need for a successful party to balance conflicting demands, which is at odds with Gehl and Porter's view, raises a second problem for the measurement of contestability. When electoral conditions favor a single party, contestability depends on the extent to which intraparty competition acts as a substitute for interparty competition. How intraparty competition is to be recognized in a contestability index is a second challenge.

6.1.5 Responsiveness

The association of competitiveness with the degree to which policy choices are responsive to the demands of citizens is one of the important ideas we pointed to in our initial discussion of the meaning of political competition. This view has a direct counterpart in a large body of empirical work that investigates how changes in the factors underlying citizen demands are reflected in changes in public policies of various kinds.

For example, Besley and Burgess (2002) consider how Indian state governments respond to falls in food production and to floods in Indian states, showing the response is greater when newspaper circulation is high and political competition, measured by differences in seat shares of major parties, is intense. Hobolt and Klemmensen (2008) use the relationship between promises in political speeches and changes in public expenditures to conclude that "higher levels of political contestation are associated with more responsive executives" (309). (Competitiveness is measured here by the proportion of the electorate that says it would vote for the governing party in the next election, a survey based measure of competitiveness that can be added to our list of indexes.) Soroka and Wlezien (2010) show that policy choices respond well to changes in what citizens want (as measured by opinion surveys) in the case of defense and social expenditures in the United States, the United Kingdom, and Canada. Kayser and Peress (2012) find that vote shares for incumbents respond positively to high levels of domestic growth and to low levels of domestic unemployment, whereas global levels of these variables have little effect, while Creedy and Moslehi (2011) use calibration of a median voter model to conclude that variation in preferences for public versus private goods plays a substantial role in explaining cross-country variation in the composition of public expenditure. Fujiwara (2015) finds that the introduction of electronic voting in Brazil effectively enfranchised less educated voters, leading to more left-wing legislators and increased spending on public health care.

This is just a small sample from an extensive literature that documents the responsiveness of policy choices to what citizens demand. An index that can be used to compare the degree of responsiveness across studies has not yet emerged from this literature.[62]

Finding that public policy is responsive to changes in the factors underlying citizen demands does not necessarily imply that the ideological positions expressed by parties or elected representatives are the same as those of the electorate (Romer and Rosenthal 1979). Politicians compromise their own interests and balance those of different voters in the pursuit of elected office. Accordingly, a branch of the responsiveness literature is concerned with measuring how well the ideological positions of political parties correspond to those of the electorate, sometimes in the context of a (still unresolved) contest between alternative electoral systems. Blais and Bodet (2006), Golder and Stramski (2010), and Rosset and Stecker (2019) are examples of studies of this kind.

6.1.6 Measuring Competitiveness between Elections

Interparty competition also arises between elections in the legislature. Two measures of competition between elections that have been well used in the empirical literature are the size of the seat majority held by the governing party or coalition and a related, discrete indicator of the minority/majority state of a parliamentary government (e.g., Ferris, Park, and Winer 2008; Gamm and Kousser 2021; Potrafke 2021). Competitiveness in the legislature will be higher when seat shares of major parties or coalitions are similar since outcomes will then be harder to manipulate and so less predictable. It will likely also be higher when a governing party does not have a simple majority of seats.

---

[62] For studies that raise doubts about the degree of responsiveness see, for example, Achen and Bartels (2016) and Matsusaka (2020). Achen and Bartels provide evidence that retrospective voting, often appealed to as a mechanism underlying responsiveness, is difficult for citizens to get right because of the problem of identifying events that are causally related to policy choices.

6.2 Does It Matter?

We complete our introduction to the empirics of political competitiveness with a sample of the research being done on its consequences. Some of the work on competitiveness as responsiveness that we have already introduced could have been included here. The applications we discuss range over a number of areas including economic growth, redistribution, government size, procurement efficiency, the business cycle, and the private good/public good composition of public expenditure. One theme running through the studies involves a chain of causation running from competitiveness to economic activity through the consequences of competitiveness for the composition of public expenditure. A wide variety of competitiveness measures are employed. This is an evolving literature.

6.2.1 Swing Voters and Economic Growth

An incumbent is less likely to win an upcoming election the larger the proportion of swing voters in the electorate is, a result shown in the Appendix. Besley, Persson, and Sturm (2010) test the hypothesis that the US Voting Rights Act of 1965 and other reforms of the period led to more growth in southern US states by increasing the proportion of swing voters who, they assume, favor policies conducive to growth relative to other policies from which they did not benefit. Using a standard growth regression with a political competitiveness index added, they show that the rise in competition after the mid-1960s is associated with more rapid growth of personal incomes. Competitiveness is measured by a variable like that recorded in Table 1 averaged over all state-wide contests for a variety of elected offices.

It is important to note that the policies favored by swing voters need not always favor growth over redistribution. For example, while Padovano and Ricciuti (2009) find that the 1995 institutional reforms in Italy that permitted greater electoral freedom in the choice of regional governors reduced political rents and increased regional incomes, the same authors (2008) find evidence at the national level in OECD countries that greater competition, measured by the first versus second party seat share margin, is inversely associated with growth, possibly because more competition leads to short-term, redistributive policy choices aimed at buying votes.

There is some evidence concerning the effects of contestability on economic growth. For example, Alfano and Baraldi (2011) consider the relationship between an HHI index of vote shares for twenty Italian regions and find an inverted U-shaped relationship with growth peaking at an HHI value of 0.3 or an *ENP* of 3.33. Analyzing Indian states, Chhibber and Nooruddin (2004) find that elections involving more than two parties, in which case, we have argued, contestability is relatively low, result in the diversion of government funds away from development activities that stimulate growth. The unresolved issue of exactly how to measure contestability hangs over these results.

6.2.2 Implications for Government Size and Procurement Efficiency

We have discussed how special interest politics and the working of the common pool problem may both lead to the growth of the public sector. Does more intense electoral competition reduce it by, for example, generating higher-quality monitoring of government programs and more effective transmission of information to voters? Or, instead, does more competition lead to larger government by exacerbating these problems? A number of empirical studies indicate that competitiveness tends to reduce public expenditure, though it is not obvious why this happens. See, for example, Rogers and Rogers (2000), Skilling and Zeckhauser (2002), Ferris, Park, and Winer (2008), Aidt et al. (2006), Aidt and Jensen (2009), Eterovic and Eterovic (2012), and Harrison, Lin, and Xu (2014). These authors each adopt a different measure of competitiveness including: the vote share received by the incumbent; a Hirschman-Herfindahl index of the proportion of time different parties were in power; the proportion of seats won by the wining party; the Polity IV index of political competitiveness across countries; and the number of years that a ruling party has been in power.

At the municipal level, Ashworth and colleagues (2014) use the number of participating parties in Flanders and vote volatility as a measure of competitiveness and Broms, Dahlstrom, and Fazekas (2019) use the propensity to use single source contract bidding in Sweden to show that the absence of competition leads to the abuse of power through the manipulation of public procurement practices. In the case of Italy, Coviello and Gagliarducci (2017) show that worse procurement outcomes at the local level are associated with longer times in office, interpreting their result as evidence that low turnover allows time for collusion with local bidders to emerge.

6.2.3 Political Competition and the Business Cycle

The claim is often made that because information about the motivation for pre-election spending and other policies is costly for voters to acquire, governing parties can use such policies opportunistically without considering their full social costs. Evidence consistent with the role of political competition in countering this decision externality arises in a number of ways. Shi and Svensson (2006) find that government budget deficits are significantly higher in developing than developed countries, a finding they attribute to the larger share of uniformed voters and lack of institutional constraints in developing countries. Even more strongly, Drazen and Eslava (2010), using a large data panel of countries find that "well informed voters not only are hard to 'buy' through spending increases but also are actually 'fiscal conservatives,' that is, they are averse to high overall government spending and deficits" (39). Within developing economies, on the other hand, Schuknecht (2000) finds evidence of expansionary fiscal policy around elections with cycles in public investment particularly prominent. Alpanda and Honig (2009) and, more recently, Aidt and colleagues (2020) look for evidence of a short-run monetary electoral cycle and find evidence within low-and middle-income countries, but "no cycle in … countries with strong political institutions" (Aidt et al. 2020, 409).

6.2.4 Competitiveness and the Private/Public Composition of the Public Expenditure

Using the multiparty, volatility-adjusted measure of closeness within constituencies discussed in Section 6.1.1, Winer and colleagues (2021) find that an increase in electoral competition was associated with changes in the composition of Indian state government budgets. In richer Indian states, more swing voters and thus greater electoral competitiveness resulted in a reallocation of state budgets from targetable private goods, such as transfers toward public goods including infrastructure, whereas in the poorest states, spending on targetable private goods grew at the expense of public goods.[63] This reinforces the view that emerges from our earlier discussion of economic growth, that while greater competition leads to policies favored by swing voters, the policies swing voters favor can differ across distinct parts of a polity.

Gamm and Kousser (2021) show that states with more equal party representation spend more on education, health, and transportation, leading to better social outcomes and higher incomes. On the other hand, Bracco, Porcelli, and Redoano (2013) find that in Italian municipalities, elected officials substitute salient taxes for those that are less salient (but not necessarily economically preferable) when political competition is tighter.

In work that includes the experience of many partially or nondemocratic regimes, Keefer and Knack (2007) show that public investment is dramatically higher in countries with low-quality governance, limited political checks and balances and no competitive elections. They interpret this as governments using public investment as a vehicle to increase their rent seeking when the quality of

---

[63] A related mechanism linking the private good–public good composition of public expenditure to the nature of the electorate is proposed and tested by Bueno de Mesquita and colleagues (2003).

governance is low. (There can be too much of a good thing!) This paper is just one of many interesting investigations of the economic consequences of alternative forms of governance in the world as a whole, a topic deserving of its own Element.

A Last Comment

The work we have reviewed shows that political competitiveness does matter and that, on balance, more of it leads to improvements in economic welfare. However, this conclusion is based on a small sample from a large and diverse literature. Moreover, even in our sample a variety of competitiveness measures have been used, each with its own time series properties and, more generally, there are conceptual issues, such as how to measure contestability, that are still unresolved.

We hope that our introduction to the empirical literature may serve as a prelude to further research on the measurement and consequences of political competition.

7 Conclusion

Economics, political science, and social choice all have well-established traditions of analysis. The challenge for those who want to work in a broader, political economy setting is to link them in a well-defined framework. We make this linkage by focusing on competition as the engine that drives the functioning of both private and public sectors, while allowing for differences in the way that it operates in these two parts of the overall structure.

Political competition lies at the center of democratic governance, just as economic competition is central for an understanding of how market economies function. In a liberal democracy, political competition accomplishes many of the distinct but related functions needed by a democratic society: it provides a way of forming and dissolving governments, it shapes and transmits the wishes of citizens, forces governments to be responsive to their demands, selects politicians and parties, and provides the stage on which interest groups struggle within rules to achieve favored outcomes.

Any political economy of public policy will acknowledge the economic context in which public resource allocation must be carried out, as we do. To incorporate its political context, our analysis focuses on the rivalry that exists among political parties in elections and between elections in the legislature. As a mechanism for the allocation of economic resources though the public sector, interparty competition is imperfect (relative to a standard defined by a perfectly competitive, well-functioning polity) for reasons that we discuss at some length.

Thus, observed policy structures are mixtures of recognizably beneficial programs and practices and others that appear harmful. Since public policies are complex equilibrium outcomes in a heterogeneous society, connecting specific features of the political process that we think lead to either "good" or "bad" outcomes with observed policy choices is a challenging task. We have done so only in some cases and at a high level of generality. Further work along these lines is a worthy endeavor.

We also consider how and why the intensity of political competition in mature democracies varies across time and space, and sample some of the interesting work that measures and investigates the implications of this variation for the structure of public policy and economic activity. There is more work to be done along these lines too.

In thinking about how to improve upon the outcomes that a competitive electoral process bequeaths to us, it is important to remember that a policy proposal cannot survive interparty rivalry and gain adoption unless voters and governments are convinced of its compatibility with political imperatives. The danger in ignoring the feasibility of a proposed policy is producing an outcome that is no longer optimal when judged from the policy designer's original standpoint if one or more parts of the program are left behind.

We should also keep in mind that, by its nature, the outcome of a competitive political process can not be known with certainty; what is compatible with an electoral equilibrium can only be known up to a probability distribution over alternatives. Moreover, policy choices and the policy process itself may be altered to some extent, albeit with costly effort, through democratic participation and institutional reform. There is considerable room for discussion and debate.

Appendix

Further Issues Concerning Behavior, Equilibrium, and the Degree of Competition

Further discussion in this Appendix of the basic model introduced in Section 3 introduces the role of valence in voting behavior, explains how the inherent instability of majority rule, for example as a result of polarization on an intensely felt issue, threatens the smooth operation of democratic choice, and illustrates how determinants of the degree of competition can be studied.

The voting density used in the probabilistic voting model introduced in Section 3 is usually written as the sum of a policy related component $v(t, G)$, and a nonpolicy or valence component ε related to ideology, assessment of party productivity, or personality and competence of the leader. The valence component is crucial for the continuity of party objectives that underlies the existence of a Nash equilibrium. If party platforms converge and the valence component of preferences is missing, any slight change in a policy platform will produce a discrete change in expected votes, and the continuity of the expected vote functions will then be lost. Valences that depend on party-specific political contributions can also be used to construct a model in which party platforms do not converge.

Assume then that each voter has a nonpolicy preference or bias for the opposition party versus the incumbent $\beta_j = \varepsilon_j^o - \varepsilon_j^i$ so that the probability that this citizen will support the incumbent can be written as

$$
\pi_j^i = \begin{cases} 1 & \text{if } v_j(s^i) - v_j(s^o) > \beta_j \\ 0 & \text{otherwise} \end{cases} \tag{A.1}
$$

with $\pi_j^o = 1 - \pi_j^i$.

The tax and spending instruments s^k may be vectors. Assume also that the party bias is a random variable from the perspective of each party with a uniform distribution over the interval $[-1/2\varphi_j, \ 1/2\varphi_j]$ such that for the incumbent $-1/2\varphi_j < v^j\left(s_j^i\right) - v^j\left(s_j^o\right) < 1/2\varphi_j$.[64] The assumption that the utility differential is contained within the bounded interval ensures that each party believes that there is always some probability, even if small, that each voter will vote for it.

---

[64] A sufficient degree of heterogeneity across voters can substitute for the use of a probability density (Lindbeck and Weibull 1987).

The last assumption is not innocuous. On some issues, voters may be so polarized that they will not support the other party under almost any circumstance, as in the pro-life versus pro-choice case. These issues are often kept out of debates on the floor of the legislature and settled in other venues such as the courts, or simply ignored. If not, in such instances expected vote functions will not be globally concave and no equilibrium may exist (Usher 1994). In other words, the probabilistic voting assumption that opens the possibility for a Nash equilibrium to exist does not banish the instability of majority rule, which continues to threaten democratic choice in this framework.

To continue, if F is the cumulative distribution of the party bias, the probability as seen by the incumbent that voter j votes for it is

$$F_j\left[v^j\left(s_j^i\right) - v^j\left(s_j^o\right)\right] = \theta_j\{(v_j^i - v_j^o) + 1/2\varphi_j\},\tag{A.2}$$

where θ_j, the derivative of F with respect to v_j^i ($= \varphi_j$ in this particular model), is the sensitivity of voter j's support for party i to a change in his or her welfare. These derivatives are the individual political influence weights in the support function (3.5). But now we see that each weight varies with uncertainty about the voter's party bias (Coughlin, Mueller, and Murrell 1990). The smaller the variance of this bias (which varies with $(1/\varphi)^2$ in the present model), the more substantial the voter's influence on the equilibrium will be.

Summing over the F_j leads to the expected vote function of each party. Enelow and Hinich (1989) and Lindbeck and Weibull (1987) consider the circumstances that lead to the concavity of this function required for the existence of a Nash equilibrium, among which is greater uncertainty about voting behavior.

If the valence terms are endogenized and differ across parties, for example because they depend on campaign contributions from partisan donors, the equilibrium will involve platform divergence. There is substantial evidence that platforms do diverge: for example, see McCarty, Poole, and Rosenthal (2016) on the United States.[65] The model of Coughlin, Mueller, and Murrell is one in which platforms may diverge and a representation theorem still applies.[66]

The role that political competition plays in this framework can be revealed more explicitly by adapting the approach of Besley, Persson, and Sturm (2010). Assume that there are just two types of voters: a fraction of voters who are committed to one of the two competing parties, $1 - \sigma$, and another fraction who are uncommitted to either party, σ, and who are identical and described by

---

[65] Stantcheva (2021) reveals polarization of voters' preferences about fiscal issues in the United States.

[66] Grofman (2004) and Schofield and colleagues (2011) discuss the divergence issue more fully.

(A.1).[67] This distinction between committed and uncommitted voters echoes the core–swing voter distinction that often appears in political science literature. (See, for example, Stokes et al. 2013, and Golden and Min 2013). Of the committed or core supporters, some fraction $(1 + \lambda)/2$ favor the incumbent, so that the fraction of all voters committed to the incumbent is $(1 - \sigma)(1 + \lambda)/2$, where λ can be positive or negative. Voters who are committed to one of the two parties vote for their chosen party independently of policies offered by the other party, while uncommitted or swing voters consider both the utility value of the programs offered by the two parties together with their party bias.

The incumbent expects to win if its expected share of all votes from committed and uncommitted voters is greater than one-half. Writing the representative swing voter's adjusted utility differential in (A.2) as $(v^i - v^o) + 1/2\theta$, where $\theta = \varphi$ and the individual subscript is omitted on the assumption that behavior is homogeneous within each voter group, this condition describing when the incumbent expects to win can be expressed (after some algebra) as

$$\left(v^i - v^o \right) + \frac{(1 - \sigma)\lambda}{\sigma\theta} \frac{\lambda}{2} > 0. \tag{A.3}$$

A highly competitive election, in the sense of being "too close to call" requires the left side to approach zero. Thus, an election becomes more competitive: (1) the larger the proportion of swing voters (the smaller is $(1 - \sigma)/\sigma$); (2) the smaller the advantage that the incumbent has in terms of committed or core supporters λ; (3) the higher is the political sensitivity of swing voters θ; and (4) the smaller is the equilibrium policy differential.

We can add to the logic underlying (A.3) by informally incorporating behavioral research about attitudes toward risk. Experimental evidence indicates that people prefer riskier choices, such as voting for a challenger rather than for the incumbent one knows well, when threatened with economic losses compared to what we would expect if we relied upon a standard expected utility theory of behavior (Quattrone and Tversky 1988). This suggests an additional reason political parties will try to avoid platforms that impose losses on sensitive or swing voters, magnifying their influence. It is not surprising, then, that swing voters play a significant role in empirical research on the consequences of competitiveness, as illustrated in Section 6.2.1.

---

[67] For a different but related model with committed and uncommitted voters, see Dixit and Londregan (1996).

References

Abdel-Khader, K., and R. De Mooij (2021). Tax Policy. In V. Cerra, B. Eichengreen, A. El-Ganainy, and M. Schindler (eds.), *How to Achieve Inclusive Growth*. Oxford Scholarship Online, 424–56. www.universitypressscholarship.com/view/10.1093/oso/9780192846938.001.0001/oso-9780192846938-chapter-12

Acemoglu, D. (2003). Why Not a Political Coase Theorem? Social Conflict, Commitment and Politics. *Journal of Comparative Economics* 31(4), 620–52.

Acemoglu, D., M. Golosov, and A. Tsyvinski (2008). Political Economy of Mechanisms. *Econometrica* 76(3), 619–41.

Acemoglu D., and J. A. Robinson (2013). Economics versus Politics: Pitfalls of Policy Advice. *Journal of Economic Perspectives* 27(2), 173–92.

Achen, C. H., and L. M. Bartels (2016). *Democracy for Realists: Why Elections Do Not Produce Responsive Government*. Princeton University Press.

Adams, J., S. Merrill, and B. Grofman (2005). *A Unified Theory of Party Competition: A Cross-National Analysis Integrating Special and Behavioral Factors*. Cambridge University Press.

Aidt, T., and P. S. Jensen (2009). Tax Structure, Size of Government, and the Extension of the Voting Franchise in Western Europe. *International Tax and Public Finance* 16(3), 362–94.

Aidt, T., and F. Magris (2006). Capital Taxation and Electoral Accountability. *European Journal of Political Economy* 22(2), 277–91.

Aidt, T., J. Dutta, and E. Loukoianova (2006). Democracy Comes to Europe: Franchise Extension and Fiscal Outcomes 1830–1938. *European Economic Review* 50(2), 249–83.

Aidt, T., Z. Asatryan, L. Badalyan, and F. Heinemann (2020). Vote Buying or (Political) Business (Cycles) as Usual? *Review of Economics and Statistics* 102(3), 409–25.

Aldrich, J. H. (1995). *Why Parties: The Origin and Transformation of Political Parties in America*. University of Chicago Press.

Alesina, A., C. Favero, and F. Giavazzi (2019). *Austerity: When It Works and When It Doesn't*. Princeton University Press.

Alfano, M. R., and L. Baraldi (2011). Political Competition and Economic Growth: Evidence from Italy. http://ssrn.com/abstract=1751066.

Allcott, H., and M. Gentzkow (2017). Social Media and Fake News in the 2016 Election. *Journal of Economic Perspectives* 31(2), 1–28.

Alpanda, S., and A. Honig (2009). The Impact of Central Bank Independence on Political Monetary Cycles in Advanced and Developing Nations. *Journal of Money Credit and Banking* 41(7), 1365–89.

Ansolabehere, S., J. M. de Figueiredo, and J. M. Snyder, Jr. (2003). Why Is There So Little Money in US Politics? *Journal of Economic Perspectives* 17 (1), 105–30.

Ashworth, J., B. Geys, B. Heyndels, and F. Wille (2014). Competition in the Political Arena and Local Government Performance. *Applied Economics* 46 (19), 2264–76.

Atkinson, A. B., and J. E. Stiglitz (1980). *Lectures on Public Economics.* McGraw-Hill.

Atkinson, M.M., H. Mou, and P. Bruce (2016). Fiscal Rules in the Canadian Provinces: Abject Failure or Qualified Success? *Canadian Public Administration* 59(4), 495–515.

Austen-Smith, D. (1987). Parties, Districts and the Spatial Theory of Elections. *Social Choice and Welfare* 4(1), 9–23.

Austen-Smith, D. (2008). Political Competition. In S. Durlauf and L. Blume (eds.), *The New Palgrave Dictionary of Economics*, 2nd ed. Palgrave Macmillan, 4982–88.

Austen-Smith, D., and T. J. Feddersen (2009). Information Aggregation and Communication in Committees. *Philosophical Transactions of the Royal Society B* 364, 763–69.

Austen-Smith, D., and J. R. Wright (1996). Theory and Evidence for Counteractive Lobbying. *American Journal of Political Science* 40(2), 543–64.

Avina, M. M., and A. Blais (2021). Are Tax Cuts Supporters Self-interested and/ or Partisan? The Case of the Tax Cuts and Jobs Act. *American Politics Research* 50(3), 416–27.

Baldwin, J. (2022). *Regulatory Failure and Renewal: The Evolution of the Natural Monopoly Contract.* A Study Prepared for the Economic Council of Canada 1989. McGill Queens' University Press.

Baqir, R. (2002). Districting and Government Overspending. *Journal of Political Economy* 110(6), 1318–54.

Bardhan, P., and T. Yang (2004). Political Competition in Economic Perspective. Working Paper E04-341. Department of Economics, University of California–Berkeley.

Bartolini, S. (1999). Collusion, Competition and Democracy: Part I. *Journal of Theoretical Politics* 11(4), 435–70.

Bartolini, S., and P. Mair (2007). *Identity, Competition and Electoral Availability: The Stabilization of European Electorates, 1885–1985.* ECPR Classics.

Basu, K. (2000). *Prelude to Political Economy: A Study of the Social and Political Foundations of Economics*. Oxford Scholarship Online. http://doi.org/10.1093/0198296711.001.0001.

Bates R. H., and D. D. Lien (1985). A Note on Taxation, Development, and Representative Government. *Politics & Society* 14(1), 53–70.

Baumol, W. J. (1982). Contestable Markets: An Uprising in the Theory of Industry Structure. *American Economic Review* 72(1), 1–15.

Becker, G. (1958). Competition and Democracy. *Journal of Law and Economics* 1, 105–9.

Becker, G. (1983). A Theory of Competition among Pressure Groups for Political Influence. *Quarterly Journal of Economics* 98(3), 371–400.

Becker, G. (1985). Public Policies, Pressure Groups, and Dead Weight Costs. *Journal of Public Economics* 28(3), 329–47.

Becker, G., and C. B. Mulligan (2003). Deadweight Costs and the Size of Government. *Journal of Law and Economics* 46(2), 293–340.

Becker, G., and C. B. Mulligan (2017). Is Voting Rational or Instrumental? In J. Hall (ed.), *Explorations in Public Sector Economics: Essays by Prominent Economists*. Springer, 1–12.

Bénassy-Quéré, A., B Coeuré, P. Jacquet, and J. Pisani-Ferry (2010). *Economic Policy: Theory and Practice*. Oxford University Press.

Beramendi, P., and D. Rueda (2007). Social Democracy Constrained: Indirect Taxation in Industrialized Democracies. *British Journal of Political Science* 37, 619–41.

Berliant, M., and M. Gouveia (2021). On the Political Economy of Income Taxation. Unpublished. MPRA paper 106138 at https://mpra.ub.uni-muenchen.de/106138/

Besley, T. (2006). *Principled Agents: The Political Economy of Good Government*. Cambridge University Press.

Besley, T., and R. Burgess (2002). The Political Economy of Government Responsiveness: Theory and Evidence from India. *Quarterly Journal of Economic* 117(4), 1415–51.

Besley, T., and A. Case (1995). Does Political Accountability Affect Economic Policy Choices? *Quarterly Journal of Economics* 100(3), 769–98.

Besley, T., and S. Coate (2003). On the Public Choice Critique of Welfare Economics. *Public Choice* 114, 253–73.

Besley, T., and T. Persson (2011). *Pillars of Prosperity: The Political Economics of Development Clusters*. Princeton University Press.

Besley, T., T. Persson, and D. M. Sturm (2010). Political Competition, Policy and Growth: Theory and Evidence from the US. *Review of Economic Studies* 77, 1329–52.

Bierbrauer, F., P. Boyer, and A. Peichl (2020). Politically Feasible Reforms of Non-linear Tax Systems. *American Economic Review* 111(1), 153–91.

Bishop, B. (2008). *The Big Sort: Why the Clustering of Like-Minded America is Tearing Us Apart*. Houghton Mifflin.

Black, D. (1958). *The Theory of Committees and Elections*. Cambridge University Press

Blais A. (2000). *To Vote or Not to Vote? The Merits and Limits of Rational Choice*. University of Pittsburgh Press.

Blais, A., and M. A. Bodet (2006). Does Proportional Representation Foster Closer Congruence Between Citizens and Policy Makers? *Comparative Political Studies* 39(10), 1243–61.

Blais, A., and I. Lago (2009). A General Measure of District Competitiveness. *Electoral Studies* 28, 94–100.

Blesse, S., F. Buhlman, and P. Doerrenberg (2021). *Attitudes towards Tax Simplification: Evidence from a Representative Survey and Experiments*. ZEW Mannheim.

Blinder, A. S. (1997). Is Government Too Political? *Foreign Affairs* 76(6), 115–26.

Boadway, R. (2002). The Role of Public Choice Considerations in Normative Public Economics. In S. L. Winer and H. Shibata (eds.), *Political Economy and Public Finance*. Edward Elgar Publishing, 47–68 (chapter), 85–97 (comments and rejoinder).

Boadway, R. (2012). *From Optimal Tax Theory to Tax Policy: Retrospective and Prospective Views*. MIT Press.

Boadway, R. (2017). Second-Best Theory: Ageing Well at Sixty. *Pacific Economic Review* 22(2), 249–70.

Boadway, R., E. Chamberlain, and C. Emmerson (2010). Taxation of Wealth and Wealth Transfers. In S. Adam, T. Besley, R. Blundell, et al. (eds.),. *Dimensions of Tax Design*. Oxford University Press, chapter 8.

Boardman, A. E., D. H. Greenberg, A. R. Vining, and D. L. Weimer (2020). Efficiency without Apology: Consideration of the Marginal Excess Tax Burden and Distributional Impacts in Benefit–Cost Analysis. *Journal of Benefit Cost Analysis* 11(3), 457–78

Bodet, M. A. (2014). Strongholds and Battlegrounds: Measuring Party Support Stability in Canada. *Canadian Journal of Political Science* 46(3), 575–96.

Bombardini, M., and F. Trebbi (2020). Empirical Models of Lobbying. *Annual Reviews of Economics* 12, 391–413.

Bowen, H. R. (1943). The Interpretation of Voting in the Allocation of Economic Resources. *Quarterly Journal of Economics* 58, 27–48.

Boxell, L., M. Gentzkow, and J. E. Shapiro (2020). Cross-Country Trends in Affective Polarization. NBER Working Paper No. 26669. https://ssrn.com/abstract=3522318.

Bracco, E., F. Porcelli, and M. Redoano (2013). Political Competition, Tax Salience and Accountability: Theory and Some Evidence from Italy. CESifo Working Paper Series No. 4167. http://dx.doi.org/10.2139/ssrn.2244783.

Bradbury, J. C., and W. M. Crain (2001). Legislative Organization and Government Spending: Cross-country Evidence. *Journal of Public Economics* 82(3), 309–25.

Brender, A., and A. Drazen (2008). How Do Budget Deficits and Economic Growth Affect Re-election Prospects? Evidence from a Large Panel of Countries. *American Economic Review* 98, 2203–20.

Brennan, G., and J. M. Buchanan (1980). *The Power to Tax: Analytical Foundations of a Fiscal Constitution*. Cambridge University Press.

Brennan, G., and L. Lomasky (1993). *Democracy and Decision: The Pure Theory of Electoral Preference*. Cambridge University Press.

Breton, A. (1996). *Competitive Governments: An Economic Theory of Politics and Public Finance*. Cambridge University Press.

Breton, A., and A. Scott (1978). *The Economic Constitution of Federal States*. University of Toronto Press.

Broms, R., C. Dahlstrom, and M. Fazekas (2019). Political Competition and Public Procurement Outcomes. *Comparative Political Studies*, 52(9), 1259–92.

Buchanan, J. (1976). Taxation in Fiscal Exchange. *Journal of Public Economics* 6, 17–29.

Buchanan, J., and R. D. Congleton (1998). *Politics by Principle, Not Interest: Towards Nondiscriminatory Democracy*. Cambridge University Press.

Buchanan, J., and G. Tullock (1962). *The Calculus of Consent: Logical Foundations of Constitutional Democracy*. University of Michigan Press.

Buchler, J. (2011). *Hiring and Firing Public Officials: Rethinking the Purpose of Elections*. Oxford University Press.

Budina, M. N., M. T. Kinda, M. A. Schnaechter, and A. Weber (2012). *Fiscal Rules at a Glance: Country Details from a New Dataset*. International Monetary Fund.

Bueno de Mesquita, B., A. Smith, R. M. Siverson and J. D. Morrow (2003). *The Logic of Political Survival*. MIT Press.

Callander, S. (2005). Electoral Competition in Heterogeneous Districts. *Journal of Political Economy* 113(5), 1116–45

Calvert, R. L. (1986). *Models of Imperfect Information in Politics*. Harwood Academic Publishers.

Caplan, B. (2001). When Is Two Better Than One? How Federalism Mitigates and Intensifies Imperfect Political Competition. *Journal of Public Economics* 80, 99–119.

Caplan, B. (2007). *The Myth of the Rational Voter: Why Democracies Choose Bad Policies*. Princeton University Press.

Capoccia, G., and D. Ziblatt (2010). The Historical Turn in Democratization Studies: A New Research Agenda for Europe and Beyond. *Comparative Political Studies* 43(8–9), 931–68.

Chen, Y. (2000). Electoral Systems, Legislative Process, and Income Taxation. *Journal of Public Economic Theory* 2(1), 71–100.

Chhibber, P., and I. Nooruddin (2004). Do Party Systems Count? The Number of Parties and Government Performance in the Indian States. Comparative *Political Studies*, 37(2), 152–87.

Coase, R. (1960). The Problem of Social Cost. *Journal of Law and Economics* 3, 1–44.

Coate, S. (2000). An Efficiency Approach to the Evaluation of Policy Changes. *Economic Journal* 110(463), 437–55.

Condorcet, Marquis de (1785). Essai sur l'application de l'analyse à la probabilité des décisions rendues à la pluralité des voix. Paris.

Congdon, W. J., J. R. Kling, and S. Mullainathan (2011). *Policy and Choice: Public Finance Through the Lens of Behavioral Economics*. The Brookings Institution.

Congleton, R. (2011). *Perfecting Parliament: Liberalism and the Rise of Western Democracy*. Cambridge University Press.

Congleton, R., B. Grofman, and S. Voigt (eds.) (2019). *The Oxford Handbook of Public Choice*. Oxford University Press.

Cordes, T., T. Kinda, P. Muthoora, and A. Weber (2017). Expenditure Rules: Effective Tools for Sound Fiscal Policy? In V. Gaspar, S. Gupta, and C. Mulas Granados (eds.), *Fiscal Politics*. International Monetary Fund, 299–325.

Coughlin, P. J. (1992). *Probabilistic Voting Theory*. Cambridge University Press.

Coughlin. P. J. (2015). Probabilistic Voting in Model of Electoral Competition. In J. C. Heckelman and R. Miller (eds.), *Handbook of Social Choice and Voting*. Edward Elgar, 218–234.

Coughlin, P. J., and S. Nitzan (1981). Electoral Outcomes with Probabilistic Voting and Nash Social Welfare Maxima. *Journal of Public Economics* 15 (1), 113–21.

Coughlin, P. J., D. C. Mueller, and P. Murrell (1990). Electoral Politics, Interest Groups, and the Size of Government. *Economic Inquiry* 28(4), 682–705.

Coviello, D., and S. Gagliarducci (2017). Tenure in Office and Public Procurement. *American Economic Journal: Economic Policy* 9(1), 59–105.

Cox, G. W., and B. R. Weingast (2018). Executive Constraint, Political Stability and Economic Growth. *Comparative Political Studies* 51(3), 279–303.

Cox, G. W., J. H. Fiva, and D. M. Smith (2019). Measuring the Competitiveness of Elections. *Political Analysis* 28(2), 168–85.

Creedy, J., and S. Moslehi (2011). *Modelling the Composition of Government Expenditure*. Edward Elgar.

Cronert, A., and P. Nyman. (2021). A General Approach to Measuring Electoral Competitiveness for Parties and Governments. *Political Analysis 29*(3), 337–55.

Cullis, J., and P. Jones (2009). *Public Finance and Public Choice: Analytical Perspectives*, 3rd ed. Oxford University Press.

Dahl, R. A. (1971). *Polyarchy: Participation and Opposition*. Yale University Press.

Dahl, R. A. (1989). *Democracy and Its Critics*. Yale University Press.

Dash, B. B., J. S. Ferris, and S. L. Winer (2019). The Measurement of Electoral Competition with Application to Indian States. *Electoral Studies* 62, 1–21.

de Figueiredo, J. M., and B. K. Richter (2014). Advancing the Empirical Research on Lobbying. *Annual Reviews of Political Science* 17, 163–85.

de Figueiredo, R. J. P. (2003). Endogenous Budget Institutions and Political Insulation: Why States Adopt the Line Item Veto. *Journal of Public Economics* 87, 677–701.

de Haan, J., R. Jong-A-Pin, and J. O. Mierau (2013). Do Budgetary Institutions Mitigate the Common Pool Problem? New Empirical Evidence for the EU. *Public Choice* 156, 423–41.

del Vicario, M., A. Bessi, F. Zollo, et al. (2016). The Spreading of Misinformation Online. *Proceedings of the National Academy of Sciences* 113(3), 554–9.

Demsetz, H. (1968). Why Regulate Utilities? *Journal of Law and Economics*, 11(1), 55–65.

Demsetz, H. (1982). *Economic, Legal, and Political Dimensions of Competition*. De Vries Lectures in Economics 4. North Holland.

Demsetz, H. (2008). The Contrast between Firms and Political Parties. In H. Demsetz, *From Economic Man to Economic System: Essays on Human Behavior and the Institutions of Capitalism*. Cambridge University Press, 130–40.

Diamond, P., and J. Mirrlees (1971a). Optimal Taxation and Public I: Production Efficiency, *American Economic Review* 61(1), 8–27.

Diamond, P., and J. Mirrlees (1971b). Optimal Taxation and Public Production II: Tax Rules, *American Economic Review* 61(3), 261–78.

Dixit, A. K. (1996). *The Making of Economic Policy: A Transaction Cost Politics Perspective*. MIT Press.

Dixit, A. K., and J. Londregan (1996). The Determinants of Success of Special Interests in Redistributive Politics. *Journal of Politics* 58(4), 1132–55.

Dixit, A., H. Grossman, and E. Helpman (1997). Common Agency and Coordination: General Theory and Application to Government Policy Making. *Journal of Political Economy* 105, 752–69.

Downs, A. (1957). *An Economic Theory of Democracy*. Harper and Row.

Drazen, A. (2000). *Political Economy in Macroeconomics*. Princeton University Press.

Drazen A., and M. Eslava (2010). Electoral Manipulation via Voter-Friendly Spending: Theory and Evidence. *Journal of Development Economics* 92(1), 39–52.

Dror, Y. (1969). The Prediction of Political Feasibility. *Futures* 1(4), 282–8.

Duverger, M. (1954). *Political Parties: Their Organization and Activity in the Modern State*. Methuen and Co.

Elkins, D (1974). The Measurement of Party Competition. *American Political Science Review*. 68(2), 682–700.

Enelow, J. M., and M. J. Hinich (1989). A General Probabilistic Spatial Theory of Elections. *Public Choice* 61(2), 101–13.

Erikson, R. S. (2015). Income Inequality and Policy Responsiveness. *Annual Reviews of Political Science* 18, 11–29.

Eterovic, D. S., and N. A. Eterovic (2012). Political Competition versus Electoral Participation: Effects on Government Size. *Economics of Governance* 13, 333–63.

Feddersen, T., and W. Pesendorfer (1997). Voting Behavior and Information Aggregation in Elections with Private Information. *Econometrica* 65(5), 1029–58

Ferejohn, J. (1986). Incumbent Performance and Electoral Control. *Public Choice* 50, 5–25.

Fernandez, R., and D. Rodrik (1991). Resistance to Reform: Status Quo Bias and the Presence of Individual Specific Uncertainty. *American Economic Review* 81, 1146–55.

Ferris, J. S., S. B. Park, and S. L. Winer (2008). Studying the Role of Political Competition in the Evolution of Government Size Over Long Horizons. *Public Choice* 137, 369–401.

Ferris, J. S., S. L. Winer, and B. Grofman (2016). The Duverger–Demsetz Perspective on Electoral Competitiveness and Fragmentation: With

Application to the Canadian Parliamentary System, 1867–2011. In M. Gallego and N. Schofield (eds.), *The Political Economy of Social Choices*. Springer Publishing, 93–122.

Fischer, S. (1980). Dynamic Inconsistency, Cooperation and the Benevolent Dissembling Government. *Journal of Economic Dynamics and Control 2*, 93–107.

Flyvbjerg, B., and D. W. Bester (2021). The Benefit–Cost Fallacy: Why Cost–Benefit Analysis is Broken and How to Fix it. *Journal of Benefit Cost Analysis* 12(3), 395–419.

Frey B. S., and A. Stutzer (2006). Mispredicting Utility and the Political Process. In E. J. McCaffery and J. Slemrod (eds.), *Behavioral Public Finance*. Russell Sage Foundation, 113–40.

Fuest, C., B. Huber, and J. Mintz (2005). Capital Mobility and Tax Competition. *Foundations and Trends in Microeconomics* 1(1), 1–62.

Fujiwara, T. (2015). Voting Technology, Political Responsiveness, and Infant Health: Evidence From Brazil. *Econometrica* 83(3), 423–64.

Galasso, V., and T. Nannicini (2011). Competing on Good Politicians. *American Political Science Review* 105(1), 79–99.

Gallagher, M., and P. Mitchel. (2009). *The Politics of Electoral Systems*. Oxford University Press.

Gamm, G., and T. Kousser (2021). Life, Literacy, and the Pursuit of Prosperity: Party Competition and Policy Outcomes in 50 States. *American Political Science Review* 115(4), 1442–63.

Gehl, K. M. and M. E. Porter (2020). *The Politics Industry: How Political Innovation Can Break Partisan Deadlock and Save Our Democracy*. Harvard Business Review Press.

Gehlbach, S. (2006). Electoral Institutions and the National Provision of Local Public Goods. *Quarterly Journal of Political Science* 2(1), 5–25.

Gerring, J., A. Hicken, D. Weitzel, and L. Cojocaru (2018). Electoral Contestation: A Comprehensive Polity-Level Analysis. V-Dem Institute Working Paper 73, University of Gothenberg.

Gerring, J., M. Palmer, J. Teorell, and D. Zarecki (2015). Demography and Democracy: A Global, District-Level Analysis of Electoral Contestation. *American Political Science Review* 109(3), 574–91.

Gilligan, T. W., and J. G. Matsusaka (1995). Deviations from Constituent Interests: The Role of Legislative Structure and Political Parties in the States. *Economic Inquiry* 33, 383–401.

Glazer, A., and L. S. Rothenberg (2001). *Why Government Succeeds and Why It Fails*. Harvard University Press.

Golden, M., and B. Min (2013). Distributive Politics around the World. *Annual Reviews of Political Science* 16, 73–99.

Golder, M., and J. Stramski (2010). Ideological Congruence and Electoral Institutions. *American Journal of Political Science* 54(1), 90–106

Gordon, S. (1999). *Controlling the State: Constitutionalism from Ancient Athens to Today*. Harvard University Press.

Graetz, M. J., and I. Shapiro (2005). *Death By a Thousand Cuts: The Fight over Taxing Inherited Wealth*. Princeton University Press.

Grofman, B. (2004). Downs and Two-Party Convergence. *Annual Reviews of Political Science* 7, 25–46.

Grofman, B., and P. Selb (2009). A Fully General Index of Political Competition. *Electoral Studies* 28(2), 291–96.

Grossman, G. M., and E. Helpman (2001). *Special Interest Politics*. MIT Press.

Grossman, G. M., and E. Helpman (2019). Electoral Competition with Fake News. NBER Working Paper #26409.

Hallerberg, M., R. R. Strauch, and J. von Hagen (2009). *Fiscal Governance in Europe*. Cambridge University Press.

Hamlin, A. (2018). What Political Philosophy Should Learn from Economics about Taxation. In M. O'Neil and S. Orr (eds.), *Taxation: Philosophical Perspectives*. Oxford University Press.

Harrison, A. E., J. Y. Lin, and L. C. Xu (2014). Explaining Africa's (Dis)Advantage. *World Development* 63(4), 59–77.

Harrison, K. (ed). (2006). *Racing to the Bottom: Provincial Interdependence in the Canadian Federation*. UBC Press.

Hartle, D. (1993). *The Federal Deficit*. Government and Competitiveness Project 93–30. School of Policy Studies, Queen's University.

Haufler, A. (2001). *Taxation in a Global Economy*. Cambridge University Press.

Hayek, F. A. (1980 [1948]). The Meaning of Competition. In F. A. Hayek (ed.), *Individualism and Economic Order*. University of Chicago Press, 92–106.

Hettich, W. (1979). Henry Simons on Taxation and the Economic System. *National Tax Journal* 32(1), 1–9.

Hettich, W. (2002). Better Than What? Policy Analysis, Collective Choice and the Standard of Reference. In S. L. Winer and H. Shibata (eds.), *Political Economy and Public Finance*. Edward Elgar Publishing, 69–84 (chapter), 85–97 (comments and rejoinder).

Hettich, W., and S. L. Winer (1988). Economic and Political Foundations of Tax Structure. *American Economic Review* 78(4), 701–12.

Hettich, W., and S. L. Winer (1999). *Democratic Choice and Taxation: A Theoretical and Empirical Analysis*. Cambridge University Press.

Hettich, W., and S. L. Winer (2006). Explaining Tax Reform. In J. Alm and M. Ryder (eds.), *The Challenges of Tax Reform in a Global Economy.* Springer, 347–61.

Hillman, A. (2019). *Public Finance and Public Policy: A Political Economy Perspective on the Responsibilities and Limitations of Government*, 3rd ed. Cambridge University Press.

Hillman, A. (1982). Declining Industries and Political-Support Protectionist Motives. *American Economic Review* 72(5), 1180–7.

Hillman, A., and H. Ursprung (2016). Where Are the Rent Seekers? *Constitutional Political Economy* 27(2), 124–41.

Hinich, M. J., and M. C. Munger (1994). *Ideology and the Theory of Political Choice.* University of Michigan Press.

Hobolt, S. B., and R. Klemmensen (2008). Government Responsiveness and Political Competition in Comparative Perspective. *Comparative Political Studies* 41, 309–37.

Hou Y., and D. L. Smith (2010). Do State Balanced Budget Requirements Matter? Testing Two Explanatory Frameworks. *Public Choice* 145, 57–79.

Hoover, K. D., and S. M. Shefrin (1992). Causation, Spending and Taxes: Sand in the Sandbox or Tax collector for the Welfare State. *American Economic Review* 82(1), 225–48.

Howitt, P. (1990). Intergenerational Redistribution. In A. Asimakopulos, R. D. Cairns, and C. Green (eds.) *Economic Theory, Welfare and the State: Essays in Honor of John C. Weldon.* McGill-Queen's University Press, 218–37.

Hsu, K. W., and C. C. Yang (2008). Political Economy and the Social Marginal Cost of Public Funds: The Case of the Meltzer-Richard Economy. *Economic Inquiry* 46(3), 401–10.

Hyde, S. D., and N. Marinov (2012). Which Elections Can Be Lost? *Political Analysis* 20(2), 191–210.

Inman, R., and D. L. Rubinfeld (2020). *Democratic Federalism: The Economics, Politics and Law of Federal Governance.* Princeton University Press.

Institute for Fiscal Studies (1977). *The Structure and Reform of Direct Taxation.* George Allen and Unwin.

Issacharoff, S., and R. H. Pildes (1998). Politics as Markets: Partisan Lockups of the Democratic Process. *Stanford Law Review* 50(3), 643–717.

Iversen, T., and D. Soskice (2006). Electoral Institutions and the Politics of Coalitions: Why Some Democracies Redistribute More Than Others. *American Political Science Review* 100(2), 165–81.

Jacobson, G. (2004). *The Politics of Congressional Elections*, 6th ed. Longman.

Jacobson, G. (2006). On Competition in US Congressional Elections. In M. P. McDonald and J. Samples (eds.), *The Marketplace of Democracy: Electoral Competition in American Politics*. Brookings Institution, 27–52.

James, S. R., A. J. Sawyer, and T. Budak (2016). *The Complexity of Tax Simplification: Experiences from Around the World*. Palgrave Macmillan.

Jones, B. D., and F. R. Baumgartner (2005). *The Politics of Attention: How Government Prioritizes Problems*. University of Chicago Press.

Kanbur, S. M. R., and G. Myles (1992). Policy Choice and Political Constraints. *European Journal of Political Economy* 8(1), 1–29.

Kangas, O. (2021). The Feasibility of Universal Basic Income. In O. Kangas, S. Jauhiainen, M. Simanainen, and M. Yikanno (eds.), *Experimenting with Unconditional Basic Income*. Edward Elgar, 187–96.

Kayser, M. A., and R. Lindstadt (2015). A Cross-National Measure of Electoral Competitiveness. *Political Analysis* 23(2), 242–53.

Kayser, M. A., and M. Peress (2012). Benchmarking across Borders: Electoral Accountability and the Necessity of Comparison. *American Political Science Review* 106(3), 661–84.

Keefer, P., and S. Knack (2007). Boondoggles, Rent-Seeking, and Political Checks and Balances: Public Investment Under Unaccountable Governments. *Review of Economics and Statistics* 89(3), 566–72.

Keen, M., and K. A. Konrad (2013). The Theory of International Tax Competition and Coordination. In A. J. Auerbach, R. Chetty, M. Feldstein, and E. Saez (eds.), *Handbook of Public Economics*. Elsevier: 257–328.

Keen, M., and B. Lockwood (2006). Is the VAT a Money Machine? *National Tax Journal* 59(4), 905–28.

Kenny, L., and S. L. Winer (2006). Tax Systems in the World: An Empirical Investigation into the Importance of Tax Bases, Collection Costs, and Political Regime. *International Tax and Public Finance* 13(2/3), 181–215.

Klein, B., and K. B. Leffler (1981). The Role of Market Forces in Assuring Contractual Performance. *Journal of Political Economy* 89(4), 615–41.

Krueger, A. (1974). The Political Economy of the Rent-Seeking Society. *American Economic Review* 64(3), 291–303

Kydland, F., and E. G. Prescott (1977). Rules Rather Than Discretion: The Inconsistency of Optimal Plans. *Journal of Political Economy* 85(3), 473–92.

Laakso, M., and R. Taagepera (1979). Effective Number of Parties: a Measure with Application to West Europe. *Comparative Political Studies* 12(1), 3–27.

Ledyard, J. O. (1984). The Pure Theory of Large Two Candidate Elections. *Public Choice* 44, 7–41.

Ledyard, J. O. (2006). Voting and Efficient Public Good Mechanisms. In B. R. Weingast and D. A. Wittman (eds.), *The Oxford Handbook of Political Economy*. Cambridge University Press, 479–501.

Ledyard, J. O. (2014). Non-coercion, Efficiency, and Incentive Compatibility in Public Goods. In J. Martinez-Vasquez and S. L. Winer (eds.), *Coercion and Social Welfare in Public Finance*. Cambridge University Press, 143–60.

Lee, D., D. Kim, and T. E. Borcherding (2013). Tax Structure and the Size of Government: Does the Value-Added Tax Increase the Size of Government? *National Tax Journal* 66(3), 541–70.

Levy, G. (2004). A Model of Political Parties. *Journal of Economic Theory* 115, 250–77.

Lin, T., J. Enelow, and H. Dorussen (1999). Equilibrium in Multicandidate Probabilistic Spatial Voting. *Public Choice* 98, 59–82.

Lindahl, E. (1919). Just Taxation – a Positive Solution. In R. A. Musgrave and A. T. Peacock (eds.), *Classics in the Theory of Public Finance*. Macmillan and Co. Ltd., 168–76.

Lindbeck, A., and J. W. Weibull (1987). Balanced-Budget Redistribution as the Outcome of Political Competition. *Public Choice* 52(3), 273–97.

Lindert, P. H. (2004). *Growing Public: Social Spending and Economic Growth since the Eighteenth Century*. 2 vols. Cambridge University Press.

Lindert, P. H. (2019). *Welfare States: Achievements and Threats*. Cambridge University Press.

Lizzeri, A., and N. Persico (2005). A Drawback of Electoral Competition. *Journal of the European Economic Association* 3(6), 1318–48.

Mandeler, M. (2012). The Fragility of Information Aggregation in Large Elections. *Games and Economic Behavior* 74, 257–68.

Marceau, M., and M. Smart (2003). Corporate Lobbying and Commitment Failure in Capital Taxation. *American Economic Review* 93(1), 241–51.

Marín, D. A., T. Goda, and G. T. Pozos (2021). Political Competition, Electoral Participation and Local Fiscal Performance. *Development Studies Research* 8(1), 24–35.

Martinez-Vazquez, J., and S. L. Winer (2014). Coercion, Welfare and Public Finance. In J. Martinez-Vazquez and S. L. Winer (eds.), *Coercion and Social Welfare in Public Finance: Economic and Political Dimensions*. Cambridge University Press, 1–26.

Matsusaka, J. G. (2020). *Let the People Rule: How Direct Democracy Can Meet the Populist Challenge*. Princeton University Press.

Mayhew, D. R. (1974). Congressional Elections: The Case of the Vanishing Marginals. *Polity* 6(3), 295–317.

McCaffery, E. J., and J. Slemrod (eds.) (2006). *Behavioral Public Finance*. Russell Sage Foundation.

McCarty, N., K. Poole, and H. Rosenthal (2016). *Polarized America: The Dance of Ideology and Unequal Riches*, 2nd ed. MIT Press.

McKee, M., and E. G. West (1981). The Theory of Second Best: A Solution in Search of a Problem. *Economic Inquiry* 19(3), 436–48.

McKelvey, R. D. (1976). Intransitivities in Multidimensional Voting Models and Some Implications for Agenda Control. *Journal of Economic Theory* 12, 472–82.

McKenzie, K. (2001). A Tragedy of the House of Commons: Political Institutions and Fiscal Policy Outcomes from a Canadian Perspective. C. D. Howe Benefactors Lecture, Toronto.

McLure Jr., C. E., and G. Zodrow (2007). Consumption-Based Direct Taxes: A Guided Tour of the Amusement Park. *Finanzarchiv* 63, 285–307.

Medina, L. F. (2007). *A Unified Theory of Collective Action and Social Change*. University of Michigan Press.

Meltsner, A. J. (1972). Political Feasibility and Policy Analysis. *Public Administration Review* 32(6), 859–67.

Meltzer, A., and S. Richard (1981). A Rational Theory of the Size of Government. *Journal of Political Economy* 89, 914–27.

Meltzer, A., and S. Richard (1983). Tests of a Rational Theory of the Size of Government. *Public Choice* 41(3), 403–18

Migué, J.-L. (1977). Controls versus Subsidies in the Economic Theory of Regulation. *Journal of Law and Economics* 20(1), 213–21.

Milesi-Ferretti, G. M., R. Perotti, and M. Rostagno (2002). Electoral Systems and Public Spending. *Quarterly Journal of Economics* 117(2), 609–57.

Miller, G., and N. Schofield (2003). Activists and Partisan Realignment in the United States. *American Political Science Review* 97, 245–60.

Mirrlees, J., S. Adam, T. Besley, R. Blundell, S. Bond, R. Chote, M. Gammie, P. Johnson, G. Myles and J.M. Poterba (2011). *Tax by Design (The Mirrlees Review)*. Oxford University Press.

Mueller, D. C. (2000). Constitutional Constraints on Governments in a Global Economy. *Constitutional Political Economy* 9, 171–86.

Mueller, D. C. (2003). *Public Choice III*. Cambridge University Press.

Musgrave, R. A. (1959) *The Theory of Public Finance*. McGraw-Hill.

Musgrave, P. (1988). Fiscal Coordination and Competition in an International Setting. In L. Eden (ed.), *Retrospectives on Public Finance*. Duke University Press, 276–305.

Nyhan, B. (2020). Facts and Myths About Misperceptions, *Journal of Economic Perspectives*. 34(3), 220–36.

Oh, J. (2017). Will Tax Reform Be Stable? *University of Pennsylvania Law Review* 165, 1159–220

Olson, M. (1982). *The Rise and Decline of Nations: Economic Growth, Stagflation and Social Rigidities*. Yale University Press.

Ostrom, E. (1990). *Governing the Commons: The Evolution of Institutions for Collective Action*. Cambridge University Press.

Padovano, F., and R. Ricciuti (2008). The Political Competition-Economic Performance Puzzle: Evidence from the OECD Countries and the Italian Regions. CESifo Working Paper 2411.

Padovano, F., and R. Ricciuti (2009). Political Competition and Economic Performance: Evidence from the Italian Regions. *Public Choice* 138(1–2), 263–77.

Palfrey, T. (1984). Spatial Equilibrium with Entry. *Review of Economic Studies* 51, 139–56.

Pareto, V. (1971 [1909]). Manual of Political Economy. A. S. Schwier (trans.). Augustus M. Kelley.

Peltzman, S. (1976). Toward a More General Theory of Economic Regulation. *Journal of Law and Economics* 19(2), 211–40.

Persson, T., and G. Tabellini (2000). *Political Economics: Explaining Economic Policy*. MIT Press.

Persson, T., and G. Tabellini (2008). Electoral Systems and Economic Policy. In B. R Weingast and D. A. Wittman (eds.), *The Oxford Handbook of Political Economy*. Oxford University Press, 723–38.

Persson, T., G. Roland, and G. Tabellini (2007). Electoral Rules and Government Spending in Parliamentary Democracies. *Quarterly Journal of Political Science* 2(2), 155–88.

Poole, K., and H. Rosenthal (1997). *Congress: A Political-economic History of Roll Call Voting*. Oxford University Press.

Popkin, S. L. (1994). *The Reasoning Voter: Communication and Persuasion in Presidential Campaigns*. University of Chicago Press.

Popper, K. (2013 [1945]). *The Open Society and Its Enemies*. One vol. ed. Princeton University Press.

Potrafke, N. (2021). Fiscal Performance of Minority Governments: New Empirical Evidence for OECD Countries. *Party Politics* 27(3), 501–14.

Profeta, P. (2002). Retirement and Social Security in a Probabilistic Voting Model. *International Tax and Public Finance* 9, 331–48.

Profeta, P., S. Scabrosetti, and S. L. Winer (2016). Wealth Transfer Taxation: An Empirical Investigation. *International Tax and Public Finance* 21(4), 720–67.

Przeworski, A. (1991). *Democracy and the Market: Political and economic reforms in Eastern Europe and Latin America*. Cambridge University Press.

Przeworski, A., and J. Sprague (1971). Concepts in Search of an Explicit Formulation: A Study in Measurement. *Midwest Journal of Political Science* 15(2), 183–218.

Quattrone, G. A., and A. Tversky (1988). Contrasting Rational and Psychological Analyses of Political Choice. *American Political Science Review* 82(3), 719–36.

Razin, A., E. Sadka, and B. Suwankiri (2011). *Migration and the Welfare State: Political Economy Policy Formation*. MIT Press.

Revelli, F., and E. Bracco. (2020). *Empirical Fiscal Federalism*. Cambridge University Press.

Riker, W. H. (1982). *Liberalism against Populism: A Confrontation Between the Theory of Democracy and the Theory of Social Choice*. W. H. Freeman and Company.

Riker, W. H. (1986). *The Art of Political Manipulation*. Yale University Press.

Riker, W. H. (1990). Heresthetic and Rhetoric in the Spatial Model. In J. M. Enelow and M. J. Hinich (eds.), *Advances in the Spatial Theory of Voting*. Cambridge University Press, 46–65.

Roberts, K. W. S. (1977). Voting over Income Tax Schedules. *Journal of Public Economics* 8, 329–40.

Roemer, J. (1998). Why the Poor Do Not Expropriate the Rich: An Old Argument in New Garb. *Journal of Public Economics* 70, 399–424.

Roemer, J. (2001). *Political Competition: Theory and Applications*. Harvard University Press.

Rogers, D. L., and J. H. Rogers (2000). Political Competition and State Government Size: Do Tighter Elections Produce Looser Budgets? *Public Choice* 105(1–2), 1–21.

Romer, T. (1975). Individual Welfare, Majority Voting, and the Properties of a Linear Income Tax. *Journal of Public Economics* 4(2), 163–85.

Romer, T., and H. Rosenthal (1979). The Elusive Median Voter. *Journal of Public Economics* 12, 143–70.

Rosset, J., and C. Stecker (2019). How Well Are Citizens Represented by Their Governments? *European Political Science Review* 11(2), 145–60.

Rubin, P. H. (2002). *Darwinian Politics: The Evolutionary Origin of Freedom*. Rutgers University Press.

Rubin, P. H. (2014). Buchanan, Economics and Politics. *Southern Economic Journal* 80(4), 912–17.

Rubin, R.H. (2019). The Capitalism Paradox: How Cooperation Enables Free Market Competition. Post Hill Press.

Rueda, D., and D. Stegmueller (2019). *Who Wants What? Redistributive Preferences in Comparative Perspective*. Cambridge University Press.

Salanié, B. (2011). *The Economics of Taxation*, 2nd ed. MIT Press.

Salmon, P. (1987). Decentralization as an Incentive Scheme. *Oxford Review of Economic Policy* 3(2), 24–43.

Salmon, P. (2019). *Yardstick Competition among Governments: Accountability and Policymaking When Citizens Look Across Borders*. Oxford University Press.

Sandler, T. (2004). *Global Collective Action*. Cambridge University Press.

Sandler, T., and D. G. Arce (2003). Pure Public Goods versus Commons: Benefit–Cost Duality. *Land Economics* 79(3), 355–68.

Sartori, G. (1976). *Parties and Party Systems. A Framework for Analysis*, vol. 1. Cambridge University Press.

Scartascini, C. G., and W. M. Crain (2021). The Size and Composition of Government Spending in Multi-Party Systems. In J. Hall and B. Khoo (eds.), *Essays on Government Growth: Political Institutions, Evolving Markets, and Technology*. Springer, 97–127.

Scheve, K., and D. Stasavage (2017). Wealth Inequality and Democracy. *Annual Reviews of Political Science* 20, 451–68.

Schofield, N. (2007). Political Equilibria with Electoral Uncertainty. *Social Choice and Welfare* 28, 461–90.

Schofield, N., C. Claassen, U. Ozdemir, and A. Zakharo (2011). Estimating the Effects of Activists in Two-Party and Multi-Party Systems: Comparing the United States and Israel. *Social Choice and Welfare* 36, 483–518.

Schuknecht, L. (2000). Fiscal Policy Cycles and Public Expenditure in Developing Countries. *Public Choice* 102, 115–30.

Schumpeter, J. (1950). *Capitalism, Socialism and Democracy*, 3rd ed. Harper and Row.

Scott, A. (1987). Tax Harmonization in the Comparison of Federal and Other States. *European Journal of Political Economy* 3(1–2), 219–49.

Seligman, E. R. A. (1921). *Essays in Taxation*, 9th ed. Macmillan.

Sen, A. (1972). Control Areas and Accounting Prices: An Approach to Economic Evaluation. *Economic Journal* 82, 486–501.

Sen, A. (1999). *Development as Freedom*. Oxford University Press.

Shafrir, E. (ed.) (2013). *The Behavioral Foundations of Public Policy*. Princeton University Press.

Sheffrin, S. (2013). *Tax Fairness and Folk Justice*. Cambridge University Press.

Shepsle, K. A. (1979). Institutional Arrangements and Equilibrium in a Multidimensional Voting Model. *American Journal of Political Science* 23, 23–57.

Shepsle, K. A., and B. R. Weingast (1981). Structure-Induced Equilibrium and Legislative Choice. *Public Choice* 37(3), 503–19.

Shi, M., and J. Svensson (2006). Political Budget Cycles: Do They Differ Across Countries and Why? *Journal of Public Finance* 90(8–9), 1367–89.

Shugart II, W. F. (1997). *Taxing Choice: The Predatory Politics of Fiscal Discrimination*. Independent Institute.

Simons, H. (1936). Rules versus Authorities in Monetary Policy. *Journal of Political Economy* 44(1), 1–30.

Simons, H. (1938). *Personal Income Taxation: The Definition of Income as a Problem of Fiscal Policy*. University of Chicago Press.

Sinn, H.-W. (2003). *The New Systems Competition*. Blackwell Publishing.

Shafrir, E. (ed.) (2013). *The Behavioral Foundations of Public Policy*. Princeton University Press.

Skaperdas, S., and S. Vaidya. (2021). Investing in Influence: How Minority Interests Can Prevail in a Democracy. CESifo Working Paper Series 9367, CESifo, Munich.

Skilling, D., and R. J. Zeckhauser (2002). Political Competition and Debt Trajectories in Japan and the OECD. *Japan and the World Economy* 14, 121–35.

Slemrod, J. (2018). Is This Tax Reform, or Just Confusion? *Journal of Economic Perspectives* 32(4), 73–96.

Sniderman, P. M., R. A. Brody, and P. E. Tetlock (1991). *Reasoning and Choice: Explorations in Political Psychology*. Cambridge University Press.

Snyder, J. M., and G. H. Kramer (1988). Fairness, Self-Interest and the Politics of the Progressive Income Tax. *Journal of Public Economics* 36(2), 197–230.

Somin, I. (2020). *Free To Move: Foot Voting, Migration, and Political Freedom*. Oxford University Press.

Soroka S. N., and C. Wlezien (2010). *Degrees of Democracy: Politics, Public Opinion and Policy*. Cambridge University Press.

Splinter, J. (2019). Electoral Competition: New Measures and Applications. PhD thesis. Carleton University.

Stantcheva, S. (2021). Understanding Tax Policy: How Do People Reason? *Quarterly Journal of Economics* 136(4) 2309–69.

Steinmo, S. (1993). *Taxation and Democracy: Swedish, British and American Approaches to Financing the Modern State*. Yale University Press.

Steinmo, S. (2003). The Evolution of Policy Ideas: Tax Policy in the 20th Century. *British Journal of Politics and International Relations* 5(2), 206–36.

Stigler, G. (1971). The Theory of Economic Regulation. *Bell Journal of Economics and Management Science* 2(1), 3–21.

Stigler, G. (1972). Economic Competition and Political Competition. *Public Choice* 13, 91–106.

Stimson, J. A., and E. M. Wager (2020). *Converging on Truth*. Cambridge University Press.

Stokes, S. C., T. Dunning, M. Nazareno, and V. Brusco (2013). *Brokers, Voters and Clientelism: The Puzzle of Distributive Politics*. Cambridge University Press.

Strom, K. (1989). Inter-party Competition in Advanced Democracies. *Journal of Theoretical Politics* 1(3), 277–300.

Strom, K. (1990). A Behavioral Theory of Competitive Political Parties. *American Journal of Political Science* 34(2), 565–98.

Sunstein, C. R. (2013). If Misfearing is the Problem, Is Cost–Benefit Analysis the Solution? In E. Shafrir (ed.), *The Behavioral Foundations of Public Policy*. Princeton University Press, 231–63.

Sunstein, C. R. (2018). *The Cost–Benefit Revolution*. MIT Press.

Sunstein, C. R. (2020). *Behavioral Science and Public Policy*. Cambridge University Press.

Surrey, S. (1973). *Pathways to Tax Reform*. Harvard University Press.

Tanzi, V. (2018). *Termites of the State: Why Complexity Leads to Inequality*. Cambridge University Press.

Thaler, R. H., and C. R. Sunstein (2008). *Nudge: Improving Decisions about Health, Wealth, and Happiness*. Penguin Books.

Theocharis, Y., and W. Lowe (2016). Does Facebook Increase Political Participation? Evidence from a Field Experiment. *Information, Communication & Society* 19(10), 1465–86.

Tiebout, C. M. (1956). A Pure Theory of Local Expenditures. *Journal of Political Economy* 64, 416–24.

Treisman, D. (2007). *The Architecture of Government: Rethinking Political Decentralization*. Cambridge University Press.

Tsebelis, G. (2002). *Veto Players: How Political Institutions Work*. Princeton University Press.

Tucker, J. A., A. Guess, P. Barberá, et al. (2018). *Social Media, Political Polarization and Political Disinformation: A Review of the Scientific Literature*. The Hewlett Foundation. https://ssrn.com/abstract=3144139.

Tucker, P. (2018). *Unelected Power: The Quest for Legitimacy in Central Banking and the Regulatory State*. Princeton University Press.

Tucker, J. A., A. Guess, P. Barberá, et al. (2018). *Social Media, Political Polarization, and Political Disinformation: A Review of the Scientific Literature*. Hewlett Foundation.

Tullock, G. (1959). Problems of Majority Voting. *Journal of Political Economy* 67(6), 571–79.

Tullock, G. (1967). The Welfare Costs of Tariffs, Monopolies, and Theft. *Western Economic Journal* 5(2), 224–32.

Ursprung, H. (1991). Economic Policies and Political Competition. In A. L. Hillman (ed.), *Markets and Politicians: Politicized Economic Choice.* Kluwer Academic Publishers, 1–26.

Usher, D. (1994). The Significance of the Probabilistic Voting Theorem. *Canadian Journal of Economics* 27(2), 433–45.

Vanberg, V. (2000). Globalization, Democracy and Citizens' Sovereignty: Can Competition Among Governments Enhance Democracy? *Constitutional Political Economy* 11(1), 87–112.

Vickrey, W. (1977). Economic Rationality and Social Choice. *Social Research* 44(4), 691–707.

von Hagen, J. (2006). Political Economy of Fiscal Institutions. In B. R. Weingast and D. A. Wittman (eds.), *The Oxford Handbook of Political Economy.* Cambridge University Press, 464–78.

Wallerstein, M. (2004). Behavioral Economics and Political Economy. *Nordic Journal of Political Economy* 30, 37–48

Warskett, G., S. L. Winer, and W. Hettich. (1998). The Complexity of Tax Structure in Competitive Political Systems. *International Tax and Public Finance* 5, 127–55

Weber, M. (1946 [1919]). Politics as a Vocation. In H. H. Gerth and C. W. Mills (eds.), *From Max Weber: Essays in Sociology.* Oxford University Press, 77–156.

Weingast, B. R., and W. Marshall (1988). The Industrial Organization of Congress; or, Why Legislatures, like Firms, Are Not Organized as Markets. *Journal of Political Economy* 96(1), 132–63.

Weingast. B. R. (1979). A Rational Perspective on Congressional Norms. *American Journal of Political Science* 23(2), 245–62.

Wellisch, D. (2000). *Theory of Public Finance in a Federal State.* Cambridge University Press.

Wicksell, K. (1896). A New Principle of Just Taxation. In R. A. Musgrave and A. T. Peacock (eds.), *Classics in the Theory of Public Finance.* Palgrave Macmillan, 72–118.

Wildasin, D. (2021). Open Economy Public Finance. *National Tax Journal* 74 (2), 467–90.

Wilson, J. D. (1999). Theories of Tax Competition. *National Tax Journal* 52(2), 269–304.

Winer, S. L. (2019). The Political Economy of Taxation: Power, Structure, Redistribution. In R. Congleton, B. Grofman, and S. Voigt (eds.), *The Oxford Handbook of Public Choice.* Oxford University Press, 456–98.

Winer, S. L., and W. Hettich (1998). What Is Missed if We Leave Out Collective Choice in the Analysis of Taxation. *National Tax Journal* 51(2), 373–89.

Winer, S. L., and H. Shibata (eds.), (2002). *Political Economy and Public Finance: The Role of Political Economy in the Theory and Practice of Public Economics*. Edward Elgar Publishing.

Winer, S. L., L. Kenny, and B. Grofman (2014). Explaining Variation in the Competitiveness of US Senate Elections, 1922–2004. *Public Choice* 161(3/4), 471–97.

Winer, S. L., J. S. Ferris, B. B. Dash, and P. Chakraborty (2021). The Privateness of Public Expenditure: A Model and Empirics for the Indian States. *International Tax and Public Finance* 28, 1430–71.

Wiseman, J. (1989). *Cost, Choice and Political Economy*. Edward Elgar.

Wittman. D. (1983). Candidate Motivation: A Synthesis of Alternative Theories. *American Political Science Review* 77(1), 142–57.

Wittman, D. (1987). Elections with N Voters, M Candidates and K Issues. In M. Holler (ed.). *The Logic of Multiparty Systems*. Kluwer Academic Publishers.

Wittman, D. (1995). *The Myth of Democratic Failure: Why Political Institutions Are Efficient*. University of Chicago Press.

Wohlgemuth, M. (1995). Economic and Political Competition in Neoclassical and Evolutionary Perspective. *Constitutional Political Economy* 6, 71–96.

Wohlgemuth, M. (2002). Democracy and Opinion Falsification: Towards a New Austrian Political Economy. *Constitutional Political Economy* 13, 223–46.

Yitzhaki, S. (1979). A Note on Optimal Taxation and Administration Costs. *American Economic Review* 69, 475–80.

Young, R. A. (1991). Tectonic Policies and Political Competition. In A. Breton, G. Galeotti, P. Salmon, and R. Wintrobe (eds.), *The Competitive State*. International Studies in Economics and Econometrics, vol 21. Springer. https://doi.org/10.1007/978-94-009-0645-7_8.

Zuboff, S. (2019). *The Age of Surveillance Capitalism: The Fight for a Human Future at the New Frontier of Power*. Public Affairs.

Acknowledgments

We are grateful to Robin Boadway, Walter Hettich, Paul Rubin, and two anonymous reviewers for their helpful comments and suggestions. We also thank James Splinter, Electoral Studies, the National Tax Journal, Oxford University Press, and Public Choice for permission to make use of some parts of previously published work. Stan Winer thanks the Center for Economic Studies at the University of Munich for the opportunity to give some lectures at an early stage in the writing of this Element. Our greatest debt is to our partners Amalia Winer and Ina Ferris.

Cambridge Elements

Public Economics

Robin Boadway
Queen's University
Robin Boadway is Emeritus Professor of Economics at Queen's University. His main research interests are in public economics, welfare economics and fiscal federalism.

Frank A. Cowell
The London School of Economics and Political Science
Frank A. Cowell is Professor of Economics at the London School of Economics. His main research interests are in inequality, mobility and the distribution of income and wealth.

Massimo Florio
University of Milan
Massimo Florio is Professor of Public Economics at the University of Milan. His main interests are in cost–benefit analysis, regional policy, privatization, public enterprise, network industries and the socioeconomic impact of research infrastructures.

About the Series
The Cambridge Elements of Public Economics provides authoritative and up-to-date reviews of core topics and recent developments in the field. It includes state-of-the-art contributions on all areas in the field. The editors are particularly interested in the new frontiers of quantitative methods in public economics, experimental approaches, behavioral public finance, empirical and theoretical analysis of the quality of government and institutions.

Cambridge Elements ≡

Public Economics

Elements in the Series

A full series listing is available at: www.cambridge.org/ElePubEcon

Printed in the United States
by Baker & Taylor Publisher Services